Drawing & Painting
The Landscape

D

The

Adrian Barlow

Quantum
Books

A QUANTUM BOOK

This book is produced by
Quantum Publishing Ltd.
6 Blundell Street
London N7 9BH

ISBN 1-86160-592-7

QUMLDP

Filmset in Great Britain by
Text Filmsetters, Orpington, Kent
Origination by
Hong Kong Graphic Arts Limited, Hong Kong

Printed in Singapore by
Star Standard Industries (Pte) Ltd.

Quarto would like to extend special thanks to
Atlantis Paper Company, Cornelissen and Son,
Falkiner Fine Papers Limited and
Langford and Hill Limited.

Contents

Introduction

Painters from most civilizations have expressed their delight in the natural world. On the walls of Egyptian tombs are innumerable images of birds, animals and flowers, painted or carved with great sympathy and displaying the result of keen observation. However, the intention of these pictures was to represent the activities and interests of man as the conqueror of nature; the plants and animals were seen as a decorative backcloth to man's presence. Although they depicted individual elements of nature in a straightforward way, Egyptian artists would never have tried to bring these elements together as a picture in the way we understand the term. They were not employed to express their own personalities, but to use colours and shapes already chosen and endowed with a particular religious meaning. The skin of men, for example, had to be red ochre, and women were always a paler shade. Backgrounds were generally white or yellow. Everything had a religious significance, so birds or plants may well have been included for symbolic reasons, even though they were painted naturalistically with strong decorative effect.

The same is true of ancient Greek paintings which were influenced, both in style and technique, by the Egyptian artist-craftsmen through the Minoan civilization. In what little painting survives from Greece, Rome and Byzantium, there is a continuing appreciation of the decorative value of natural forms, but to most people at that time, nature must have represented sheer physical hard work, rather than an object of intrinsic beauty.

In medieval art, nature takes on a greater symbolic value and is represented less realistically. Artists worked in the service of Christianity, a religion which in its early centuries scorned sensuality. There was a considerable fear of nature, of dark forests, storms and other natural hazards, perhaps reflecting a fear of man's own nature. In paintings of this period, a single stylized tree might be used to represent the whole Garden of Eden.

Gradually, however, nature was seen to be tamed in the monastery gardens, and even eventually associated with enjoyment. Later medieval poetry extolled pleasures which were decidedly un-Christian in the sense of the earlier religious teachings, and these ideas later found a pictorial expression in the work of the Italian Renaissance. There is little vegetation in evidence in the great pioneering frescoes of Giotto (1267-1337), but wonderful glimpses of the natural world can be seen in the paintings of the later Sienese school – particularly in *Good and Bad Government* by Ambrogio Lorenzetti (1319-1398) and some works by Simone Martini, who was a friend of the poet Petrarch (1304-1374).

The landscape played an increasingly important role in painting, albeit with strong human associations, and by the time of Piero della Francesca (1410/20-1492) the figures are inseparable from their natural surroundings. A good example of this is a small work by this artist in the Accademia in Venice, *St Jerome and a Devotee*. It shows an interesting use of colour which conveys a strong bond between man and his environment. The landscape is painted in soft

Right A wall painting from the tomb of Semmejem, Egypt. Dating from the time of the New Kingdom (1580-1085 B.C.), it depicts the agricultural products of the river Nile and shows an awareness of the rich decorative value of natural forms. One of the purposes of such paintings was to ensure the deceased was supplied with adequate provisions for the afterlife, demonstrating a remarkable belief in the power of visual imagery. The artists who were entrusted with this task could clearly not resist the opportunity to exploit the decorative potential of the trees, the corn and the patterned animal. The water, too, is expressed as a decorative surround.

greens and umbers. The figure of St Jerome, a wooden crucifix and the town behind are painted in a similar, but lighter range of colour. The effect of this is to establish immediately a relationship between the saint and the landscape where he is evidently at home. The devotee, however, is clearly a visitor, as expressed by the isolated cool red of his cloak, its colour making a delicate balance with the complementary greens behind. The painting has a Christian theme, but nature is no longer treated symbolically but is represented as a cultivated and unthreatening setting.

This and other paintings demonstrate that Piero had a profound feeling for geometry and a developed appreciation for the laws of perspective. He also made extensive use of a canon of geometric proportion derived from Pythagoras and known today as the

Golden Section. Commonly applied in classical Greek architecture, it is based on the idea that certain relationships of shapes are especially satisfying to the eye. Its laws are derived from forms in nature, such as the spirals found in sea shells and the way seeds are placed in sunflower heads, and the rectangle based on such forms has been used by many artists during and since the Renaissance. Good examples of Piero's use of the Golden Section are the *Flagellation* (1456/7) in Urbino and the *Baptism* (usually considered one of his earliest works) in the National Gallery, London. The latter picture is still not a "pure" landscape, as the figures are the most significant elements, but from the flowers in the foreground to the fields on the horizon, all is closely and objectively observed. There are no strong contrasts of light and shade, no apparent literary overtones, a carefully considered use of colour (note how the eye is led into the background by the alternate coloured and monochromatic figures); all conspiring to give the utmost clarity.

Another example of straightforward observation of landscape, a little later in the fifteenth century, is the work of Giovanni Bellini (1430/40-1516). His paintings show a greater interest in light and shade, while there is an attempt to convey the feeling of a particular time of day, which did not seem to interest Piero della Francesca so much. In many ways, the work of these two painters can be seen as examples of a tradition of landscape painting (a cool, direct and uncluttered observation of the world) which was later continued by such painters as Bruegel, members of the Dutch school and, to some extent, by the Italian painter Canaletto.

A different tradition of landscape painting began

Left A drawing by a monk, (c.1066). The tree forms betray little interest in objective observation, but serve as a general symbol of nature. In much medieval art there are strong patterns derived from flora and fauna but the landscape as a whole was not seen as a fit subject for the artist.

with Italian painters such as Giorgione (1475-1510). Together with the Renaissance interest in classical sculpture, there existed an equal interest in the Latin poetry of Ovid and Virgil, who had themselves been influenced by the Greek writers Theocritus and Hesiod. The idea of a Golden Age of pastoral bliss, described anew in a work called *Arcadia* (1504) by Jacopo Sannazaro increasingly appealed to the Renaissance artists. Many branches of the arts have been influenced, directly or indirectly, by this work – Shakespeare's *As You Like It*, for example – but most of all, landscape painters. The word Arcadia is still used to evoke an earthly paradise.

Giorgione's *Fête Champêtre* (c.1510) is a visual expression of this ideal landscape. The composition is again dominated by figures but the countryside is more than a background. The effect of the picture is very dependent on the way in which nature is represented. The light and shade in the trees, the delicate foliage, the distant glimpse of the sea, all reinforce the lyrical mood of the lovers. This picture is not just an ideal landscape, it also suggests an ideal climate in which the arts can flourish.

Some 35 years after Giorgione's death, one of the greatest landscape painters was working in northern Europe; Pieter Bruegel (1525-1569). His pictures follow the more naturalistic tradition of Piero della Francesca rather than the poetic idealism of Giorgione and Titian. He does refer to classical literature in *The Fall of Icarus* (c.1558), but even in this picture, the figure of Icarus falling into the sea plays a very small part in the composition, which is a wonderful panoramic landscape. Bruegel chose to paint this scene as an illustration of the German proverb "no plough comes to a standstill because a man dies" – a down-to-earth expression summing up human indifference. His treatment of the theme shows his preoccupation with everyday life.

Among Bruegel's other landscapes are a series depicting the four seasons. They do not have the geometric balance that can be seen in Piero's work but their composition is by no means haphazard. In *The Hunters in the Snow* (c.1565) a line of trees is placed in a perfect row down the hillside, creating a strong link between the returning hunters in the foreground and the skaters below. This downward movement is again emphasized by the diagonals of the hunters' spears, the steep roofs on the left and the swooping bird. In *The Corn Harvest* there is again much repetition of shapes. The eye is led from the standing corn in the foreground to the fields in the distance, by a broad sweep which continues back along a cart track to the left of the picture. The conical forms of the women's hats mirror the stooks of corn, and the brace of partridge to the left are echoed by the figures behind them carrying sheaves.

Bruegel's use of colour is interesting, too, helping to achieve the overall clarity to be observed in Piero della Francesca's paintings. The group of peasants having their midday meal at the foot of a tree demonstrates how colour is used to augment form. The colours of the clothing match the peasants' gestures of eating and drinking, and their sense of fulfilment. The quality of the bread which the woman with her back to us is eating is conveyed in the colour of her blouse and hat, a colour which is derived from the surrounding corn. The man at the back must be drinking wine, judging by the colour of his shirt. We can feel his thirst in this colour. The position of white in the clothing of the other figures reinforces the ways they are eating their white broth. The prostrate man on the left has obviously had his fill of both broth and wine, as conveyed by his white shirt and the wine-coloured cloth under his head. This use of local colour is a subtle way of portraying atmosphere and temperature.

The traditions founded by Giorgione were continued in Italy by Claude Lorraine (1600-1682), born in France, but an Italian painter by adoption. He first went to Rome as a pastrycook, but went on to study painting there and his idealized scenes of antiquity have been an enduring influence on landscape artists. Although Claude, like Bruegel, has been described as a simple man, his work suggests otherwise. Claude's compatriot and near-contemporary, Nicolas Poussin (1594-1665), who also lived in Rome where the two artists went out painting together, was certainly more educated and his paintings have a more obvious intellectual content. Both painters took up the theme of Arcadia, Claude more exclusively in terms of the ideal landscape, Poussin hinting at nature's darker side. A characteristic work by Poussin, copied from Guercino (1591-1666), is *Et in Arcadia Ego*, meaning "Even in Arcadia I (death) am found". Romantics were later to misinterpret this as "I, too, have tasted Paradise", but Poussin's message was less simple.

Claude often worked directly from nature, and, although his themes were classical, his real interest was light. He is known for his magnificent sunsets and also for effects of light at all times of the day. Where other landscape painters observed the effects

of the different seasons on the countryside, he portrayed the changing light from dawn to dusk. His drawings show great freshness and immediacy, although his finished paintings seem to follow a formula in their composition. There is generally a dark foreground, a large clump of trees or group of buildings on one side, a smaller one on the other side, a paler middle distance and then a glorious sky full of infinite nuances of light. His eye for subtle changes of tone enabled him to present vast areas of sky and immense distances, often without using particularly bright colours. As a result his work unfortunately does not reproduce very well.

Claude and Poussin made an enormous impression on the eighteenth-century English painters, Constable, Girtin and Turner. One of Claude's greatest and most influential paintings was *Psyche at the Palace of Cupid* (*c*.1664), an idea taken from a tale in *The Golden Ass*, written by the late Roman writer Apuleius (*b*.A.D.125). The painting is full of poetry and has quite understandably been known as *The Enchanted Castle*, a classic example of the Arcadian theme. Turner said of one of Claude's paintings that

Above *Fête Champêtre* (*c*.1510), Giorgione. His life was short and barely a dozen works survive. Giorgione was a Venetian, a pupil of Giovanni Bellini, and this work shows him as one of the first painters to express a mood by means of a landscape. He was also one of the first Venetians to paint pictures for private collectors, which were executed on a smaller scale than work intended for churches. It was not unusual at the time for works which were left unfinished to be completed by another artist. It is thought that Titian finished this one when Giorgione died of the plague. It expresses the youthful hopes of the Renaissance itself.

he was both pleased and unhappy when he viewed it – it seemed to be beyond the power of imitation. But Poussin, with his rigorous use of geometry and the Golden Section, with strong right-angles and frontal compositions, was less popular with the English. Poussin was more the precursor of the strongly structured landscapes of Cézanne.

Well before Claude's death in 1682, pure landscape had come to be seen as a fit subject by artists all over Europe. There was already a wealth of naturalistic painting in Holland – Jan van Goyen (1596-1656), Jacob van Ruisdael (1628/9-1682), Adraien van de Velde (1636-1672), Meindert Hobbema (1638-1709), not to mention Rubens (1577-1640) and Rembrandt (1606-1669). Landscape was, however, subordinate to Rubens' flamboyant historical and mythological subjects and Rembrandt's profound humanitarian vision, although Rembrandt's unsurpassed skill as a draughtsman can be seen in innumerable landscape etchings and drawings. One painting by Rembrandt which does treat landscape as a major theme is the *Landscape with an Obelisk*, a dramatic, imaginative work about the forces of nature.

Right *The Baptism of Christ*, Piero della Francesca. There are few paintings which have so fully captured the calm, impersonal beauty which is often associated with the best classical sculpture. This unemotional view of the world owes much to Piero's love of geometry. The principal lines in the composition follow harmonic proportions based on the Golden Section.

Left *Et in Arcadia Ego* (1639-40), Nicholas Poussin; one of two copies Poussin made of a painting of the same title by Guercino. The inevitability of death was a constant theme in classical Greek and Roman literature. This theme is used here ironically by Poussin, with his reference to Arcadia on the tomb, and the idealized landscape setting.

Below *The Corn Harvest* (c. 1565), Pieter Bruegel; one of a series of five paintings depicting the seasons of the year. In all these pictures he expresses his love of the countryside and the close relationship between man and his surroundings. All of them contain figures of country people, whose labours he celebrates, but the important features of the composition are always dominated by the landscape. Although he may seem to have romanticized rural life, he did not seek the lyrical mood to be found in Giorgione's *Fête Champêtre*. Rather, he appears to be satisfying his curiosity and delight in agricultural practices. With Breugel the realistic landscape emerges as a noble theme.

Jacob van Ruisdael, who died the same year as Claude, stands out as one of the greatest painters of the realistic northern school. His output was enormous, and his later work shows a more romantic vein than others of this period, with large skies and sweeping clouds casting deep shadows across the fields. He was much admired by Constable.

It was not until the middle of the eighteenth century that landscape painting developed in England into something more than topographical views of country estates. In 1746, Canaletto (1697-1768) came to England from Venice in search of more patronage. He is best known for his views of Venice painted to sell to gentlemen on the Grand Tour, mostly English, but when he seems to have been painting more for himself, as in *The Stonebreaker's Yard* and *The View of Whitehall looking North*, he displayed his full powers of observation.

Canaletto made some use of a *camera obscura*, which had been invented in the sixteenth century although the basic principle was noted by Aristotle: The *camera obscura* is a box with a lens at the front, an inclined mirror inside and a glass screen on top, over which is placed a sheet of thin paper. If the scene is

Above *Psyche at the Palace of Cupid*, Claude Lorraine; an idealized landscape but nevertheless the result of innumerable studies direct from nature. The figure plays an insignificant part in the compositional structure of the work, despite its importance for the content.

As already suggested, Claude was a major influence, but English painters added a quality of their own – a more personal, less academic response to the countryside. Richard Wilson (1714-1782), Sir Joshua Reynolds, George Stubbs (1724-1806), Joseph Wright (1734-1797) and John Cozens (1752-1797) all made the pilgrimage to Italy, although they did not embrace its influence to the same degree. Stubbs and Wright refused to acknowledge the authority of the academic doctrines of the past, as did Thomas Gainsborough (1727-1788) who never left his native country. The determination of these artists to take a fresh look at nature introduced an important element into the art of the period, resulting in a complex interaction between the academic approach and a more spontaneous response to the visual world.

Gainsborough made a very individual and unorthodox contribution with freely drawn and rather emotional evocations of landscapes. He painted portraits for a living, but wrote to a friend, "I'm sick of portraits, and wish very much to take my Viol da Gamba and walk off to some sweet village when I can paint landscapes and enjoy the fag end of life in quietness and ease." This wishful thinking recalls Giorgione's *Fête Champêtre*. The influence of classical art and literature, the beginnings of industrialization in the cities, all gave impetus to the image of Arcadian release.

Towards the end of the eighteenth century three artists were born within a year of each other: Thomas Girtin, William Turner (1775-1851) and John Constable (1776-1837); the latter two becoming the greatest English landscape painters. Girtin is best known for his watercolours, a medium in which he made considerable innovations, using richer, more direct application. He died in his late twenties; Turner said, "If Tom Girtin had lived I should have starved." Turner worked in a great variety of media and tackled an enormous range of themes, whereas Constable devoted himself almost exclusively to an honest, naturalistic observation of the English countryside.

Both Turner and Constable were admirers of Claude, and in Constable's work this influence was finally assimilated with the equally strong influence of the Dutch painter Ruisdael. Constable concentrated on the particular sensations received from a particular scene in nature, where Claude had taken elements from different places and welded them into an imaginative composition. Some comparisons can also be made between Constable and the poet Wordsworth. Each loved the familiar and never turned their back on the countryside where they grew up. Both were important figures in the Romantic movement which took place between about 1750 and 1850, and much of Wordsworth's poetry could be describing Constable's painting, as this example from *Tintern Abbey*:

I have learned
To look on Nature, not as in the
Hour of thoughtless youth; but hearing oftentimes
The still, sad music of humanity.

There was certainly an element of sadness, even

sufficiently bright it will be projected onto the paper which can then be traced. In the early days of its use, when lenses were of relatively poor quality, the image was distorted at the edges, and not all artists who used it as a drawing aid thought to correct this distortion. Among English painters to have used it are the Sandbys, Paul (1725/6-1809) and Thomas (1721-1798), de Loutherbourg (1740-1812), Thomas Girtin (1775-1802) and John Crome (1768-1821). Sir Joshua Reynolds (1723-1792) had a folding model, bound to look like a book on ancient history.

Another curious optical toy which should have a brief mention in the history of landscape painting is the "Claude glass", more for its indication of the influence of Claude on the English than for any practical usefulness it might have had. The Claude glass was a curved, tinted mirror which was supposed to turn a reflection of a hilly landscape at sunset into a Claude painting. The reflection subdued colours so that the subject was seen in light and shade. These glasses were very popular with travellers and romantic poets.

Canaletto's move to England was typical of a general trend among Italian artists looking for wealthier clients. The flourishing of the arts has always been closely linked with, if not entirely dependent on, the existence of rich patrons. While England's wealth was increasing, Italy's was declining, although there was an element of exchange between the countries. An interest in classical values in art was an important reason why a rich young Englishman's education was not considered complete in the eighteenth century until he had made a Grand Tour of Europe, the climax of which was a prolonged stay in Italy. So the great flowering of landscape painting in England was backed by a growing prosperity, from the industrial revolution, and an extensive knowledge of earlier European traditions.

Above *Wheatfields (c. 1650)*, Jacob van Ruisdael. This artist was a contemporary of Claude, but had more sympathy for the tradition of realism. Where Claude's art was lyrical and Mediterranean, with literary associations, Ruisdael's was realistic and Northern. Despite an enormous output, Ruisdael is said to have been a dour man who never painted a clear and sunny day. Nevertheless, his paintings are not entirely lacking in romanticism.
Left *Landscape with an Obelisk* (c. 1638), Rembrandt. This is one of the few paintings by this master with landscape the dominant theme. The scale of the figures serves to intensify the drama and storminess of the landscape.

Left *View of Whitehall Looking North* (c.1730), Antonio Canaletto Canaletto is probably best known for his views of the canals and buildings of Venice. He often painted at great speed for the tourist market. He was certainly skilful and, at his best, a thoughtful and objective observer in a realistic tradition. His earlier Venetian scenes were painted on the spot, which was unusual at the time, but he later worked both from drawings and with a *camera obscura* in the studio. He worked in England for about ten years in the mid-eighteenth century.

pessimism, in Constable's later work, and there may well have been an element of nostalgia, for by the 1820s there was much unemployment and poverty in country life which he would not have been affected by as a child. But it was his interest in the familiar which gave his work its strength. He would work extensively from the same view before attempting the finished canvas. First he made rapid pencil drawings in note-books, followed by rapid paintings in oil, then more detailed drawings and larger paintings. One of his many qualities was an ability to hold on to his original conception of the work and develop and refine it by constant study. He even made full-sized paintings for himself before proceeding to the finished version to be exhibited. Perhaps he felt a need to conform to the contemporary notion of what constituted a "finished" picture, but the immediacy of his prepara-tory works is often more appealing now. It is interest-ing to look at the finished *View of Hampstead Heath* beside the study for that work. The latter is painted much more freely with quick broad brushstrokes. In some of his more highly finished works he did gain additional richness from the inclusion of greater detail, but sometimes overdid it by putting little flecks of light on almost every leaf. This does not detract from his achievements. His paintings were about the countryside, but also about enjoying being there. Most importantly, they were the result of a direct relationship with what he saw before him.

Where Constable concentrated his attention on familiar landscapes, Turner had much wider in-terests in terms of subject-matter. He started his career using watercolours, working alongside Thomas Girtin on fairly traditional landscapes, and although he later painted a lot with oils, he contrived to use this medium throughout his life. It could be said that his oil paintings were influenced by this understanding of watercolour, a medium well suited to his interest in high-key effects of light. Water-colour does not give a tonal range at all comparable with oil paint, and Turner's oil paintings mostly employed the brighter part of the spectrum, often in conjunction with pure white, giving a similar effect to watercolour paper. This love of brightness was not fully expressed in his work until he eventually went to Italy at the age of 44, by which time he had established a controversial reputation for himself with the bold "unfinished" look of his pictures.

Turner's taste for the romantic and dramatic can be seen in his grand themes. In *Snow Storm, Hannibal crossing the Alps*, and in most of the storm and shipwreck pictures, the violence of nature is the real theme. In *Hannibal* the soldiers display no heroics but crouch sensibly behind rocks. The composition of the painting is similarly unclassical with its diagonal sweeps and the absence of vertical and horizontal lines; nature is presented in disorder. Dark, pessimistic streaks in his character were challenging the more serene classical influences Turner had admired as a young man. His delight on arriving in Venice for the first time, was not so much due to the magnificent architecture and pictures, but was an appreciation of the glare of the sky and the reflections in the lagoon.

Conventional taste had found trends in Turner's work difficult to appreciate earlier, and it was to be increasingly perplexed. His works had already been labelled by contemporary critics as "pictures of nothing, and very like". Another quip – "tinted steam" – was probably generally accepted as fair comment. Turner did, however, have a champion in the writer John Ruskin (1819-1900), who extolled the art of landscape painting, particularly Turner's. Unfortunately, Ruskin got carried away by his belief in Turner as the greatest of landscape painters, and is thought to have destroyed, on Turner's death, a number of figure drawings which Ruskin considered pornographic and harmful to Turner's reputation. The breadth of Turner's vision was misunderstood even by the person who did most to advance him.

Turner did not actually settle in Venice for any length of time but made hundreds of watercolour studies there, painting in oil on his return to England.

Left *The Leaping Horse*, John Constable. Constable absorbed both southern and northern influences: he admired both Claude and Ruisdael. He had a strong, intuitive feeling for composition, and for the part played in his pictures by the contrast of light and shade. The study for *The Leaping Horse* (above) is almost exactly the same size as the finished work, but there are some important differences. In the study, the activities of the boatmen tend to attract our interest away from the horse; in the finished work the boatmen play a more passive role, with the result that our eyes revert to the horse more quickly. Constable felt the need for a diagonal accent to echo the movement of the horse on the far side of the river to the left, so although the oar is dispensed with, the accent is retained in a furled sail. By moving the small tree to the left of the horse, the vista to the right is opened up and becomes characteristically more romantic.

There is little recognizable form in the paintings, the composition depending entirely on the juxtaposition of colours. He was not really attempting to paint the effect of light, but to paint light itself.

Well before Turner's death in 1851, it had become accepted for a landscape painter to work directly from the subject, rather than make studies outside and then compose a picture from them in the studio. A school more or less devoted to the outdoor approach developed in Norwich. This part of England had strong trade links with Holland and many Dutch paintings had found their way into East Anglian collections. It was natural that artists here should absorb the influence of Ruisdael, Hobbema and Aelbert Cuyp (1620-1691), all the more so as the countryside was similarly flat. The principal figures of the Norwich school were John Crome and John Sell Cotman (1782-1842). They painted landscapes in watercolour and oil with great freshness, following the Dutch tradition of enjoyment of the familiar scene.

The hundred years preceding Turner's death in 1851, had seen great developments. At the beginning of this period, the creative energy was in part the result of the successes of England as a country, and these successes saw the growth of a middle class which could afford paintings. A painter could survive without the patronage of an aristocracy educated on the classics. Both Constable and Turner had been nurtured on Claude but subsequently developed individual styles. However, neither was immensely popular at his death. Constable was born relatively poor and died in a similar condition, his work not fully appreciated in his own country. Turner enjoyed worldly success – he was a shrewder man – but his later work had no immediate influence.

Although he had little following in England, Constable was much admired in France, where he had exhibited *The Hay Wain* and the *View on the Stour* in 1824. The romantic painters, Géricault (1791-1824) and Eugene Delacroix (1798-1863), travelled to England where they welcomed the change from the classical traditions still prevalent in their own country. It was Constable's free handling of paint that impressed Delacroix, rather than his subject matter, but both of these aspects were later to have an influence on Jean Francois Millet (1814-1875), Diaz de la Peña (1807-1876) and Theodore Rousseau (1812-1867). These three formed a group of landscape painters at Barbizon, in the country south of Paris. In common with Constable, their work was based on the direct observation of rural life. Millet at his best had a wonderful eye for colour in which he anticipates Impressionism. The group as a whole upheld the dignity of peasant labour, but tended to sentimentalize.

It was not only the influences from England at this time that produced great landscape artists. Jean Baptiste Camille Corot (1796-1875) showed little interest in either Constable or the Romantic movement in general. He was born in Paris and made a late start in painting as his father wanted him to go into the family drapery business. He was a generous, ingenuous

man, always charitable to other artists, and ready to help and learn from the young. This openness is seen in his painting, through his ability to simplify and rationalize forms without generalizing them. Combined with this was a natural gift for the very accurate observations of tonal values. He often used a full tonal range, from very dark to very light, with intermediate colours carefully evaluated within the overall tonal structure. In many of his landscapes, he chose a time of day when shadows are deep and the sunlight only picks out a few areas brightly, often making these few light shapes the focus of our interest. A particularly good example is *The Lake of Geneva: The Quai des Paquis* where it seems he has made an early decision in its composition about which few shapes will be the brightest.

Corot's training was classical, following in Claude's and Poussin's footsteps to Rome. As was now common practice, he made small paintings from nature with the intention of using them for larger

Above *Venice* (1840), J.M.W. Turner. This is one of Turner's more elaborate compositions in praise of the rich effects of light which he found so compelling in the city. Compared with his later paintings of Venice, this contains a wealth of detail; this was subsequently to dissolve into the bright mists of the lagoon in later works.

Right *Appledore*, Thomas Girtin. In this watercolour of a river estuary very few colours are used and none of them are very bright; it is Girtin's extensive use of very watery paint which gives the work its expressive quality.

works to be completed during the winter months. In these small studies he displayed a sure sense of composition, and an accurate eye for tone and colour. In other words, his studies were complete works on their own, and they remain his best work. Where he went on to enlarge one of these little paintings into an exhibition piece he frequently failed, simply because the initial quality of his on-the-spot observation was the real core of his work: in these studies, he wanted to capture precise moments of the day when the tonal structure was of critical importance. He said, "Never leave anything uncertain in whatever you do. Paint the picture part by part, as fully as possible at the first try, so that very little remains to be done after everything has been covered with paint. I have observed that something done at the first attempt is more direct, more attractive, and that it is often possible to take advantage of accidents; whereas if one does a thing over, one often loses the original colour harmony."

Constable's landscapes expressed an underlying philosophy about man's relationship with nature, but Corot's were the result of a more direct, less literary response. Yet it could be claimed that both painters were important forerunners of Impressionism because their best work was done while they were actually looking at the motif – the physiological eye was playing a greater role in the construction of the picture. Looking back to the painting of Claude, Bruegel or Piero della Francesca, it is apparent that their grand and ambitious themes could never have been achieved without painstaking studio preparation. It would be unfair to Corot to say that he was less ambitious in his work than these masters, for *his* visual explorations were in relatively new territory. He could have pointed out quite correctly that the Umbrian sun would never have cast such pale and delicate shadows as those we see under Piero's trees. Both Corot and Constable shared a part in the trend towards visual realism.

By the middle of the nineteenth century Europe was no longer the only place where Western landscape traditions were emerging and being adapted. In America, Washington Allston (1779-1843) and Thomas Cole (1801-1848), the most important painters of the Hudson River school, had imported a Claudian approach, which they both developed into a more extravagantly romantic style, similar to their English contemporary John ("Mad") Martin (1789-1854). Cole had grown up in England and, after emigrating to America, continued to travel in the West Indies and Europe throughout his life. When in Italy he rented the studio which was thought to have belonged to Claude.

The continuing admiration of Claude was also manifest in the work of early Australian painters, John Glover (1767-1849), for example. However, at this time the Australian population was still tiny, in part composed of people who were there against their will. It was not until the Swiss painter Louis Burelot arrived in 1864, bringing with him the open-air techniques of the Barbizon school, that an important Australian movement got under way.

Below *Snow Storm: Hannibal and his Army Crossing the Alps (1812),* J.M.W. Turner. This imaginative composition shows a mixture of romanticism and worldliness. The dramas of nature form the real subject, and Turner no doubt enjoyed the irony that the soldiers survived the passage only to suffer a more tedious defeat in Italy.

Bottom *Golden Summer* (1888), David Davis. Davis was one of the Australian artists who were indirectly influenced by the Barbizon school in France. He took part in an exhibition held in Melbourne in 1889, called the 9 x 5 exhibition because all the works were painted on wooden cigar box lids of those dimensions. Many of the paintings were of the countryside around Melbourne.

Above *Avignon: View from Villeneuve* (1835), Jean-Baptiste Camille Corot. This is one of many small landscapes painted out of doors by Corot during his summer travels. He kept it in his own collection all his life He may well have considered it as a study for a larger work to be completed in the winter months, but the composition is so satisfactory that it is hard to imagine how a different scale might improve it. There is a close relationship between the way in which an artist makes his observations and the scale whereby he translates them into paint.

It was in France that the greatest changes were taking place, accelerating the progress of natural realism, a trend anticipated by the preceding generation of artists. Gustave Courbet (1819-77) condemned romanticism along with classicism, reacting against the idealization of nature which was current teaching in the art schools and considerably debased. Only the familiar was worth the artist's attention: "Nature offers a beauty superior to any artistic convention." His work was uneven in quality, but his fierce stand against academism set an example for the Impressionists, who spent a large part of their lives as poor and unpopular as Courbet.

The main figures of the Impressionist movement, Camille Pissarro (1831-1903), Edouard Manet (1832-83), Edgar Degas (1834-1917), Paul Cézanne (1839-1906), Alfred Sisley (1839-99), Claude Monet (1840-1926) and Auguste Renoir (1841-1919) were all born between 1831 and 1841. Of these, Manet and Degas were neither landscape painters, nor entirely Impressionist in their own work, but must be mentioned for their influence and support for the group. Cézanne and Renoir also developed away from the movement after its initial achievements, but for a time the paintings of all of them represented an explosive reaction to the increasingly dry and colourless work of the academic school. Pissarro, Sisley and

Monet took natural realism to an ultimate point, excluding any element which was not informed by the visual impression received by the eye. Paintings were executed in front of the subject, often a familiar landscape, a street or a river scene, pitched in a high key, with bright colours discovered even in the deepest shadows.

One of the Impressionists' most durable achievements was to show that anything can be a fit subject for painting; the importance lay not with what was painted but how it was perceived. Monet, starting from the direct influence of Corot and the very indirect influence of Constable, went on to choose the formal facades of cathedrals and the almost formless shapes of haystacks to demonstrate this point.

Renoir was a close associate of Monet for a while, but after some success with portrait paintings, he travelled around Europe, studying in museums, and became increasingly dissatisfied with the limitations of Monet's exclusively visual approach. Sisley, like Monet, remained true to the ideals of Impressionism, but somehow with less conviction and his later paintings suffered as a result. Pissarro, in his old age, began to introduce into his work a more conscious structure than we see in the very freely composed waterlily paintings of Monet; indeed both of them, by the 1890s, were debating to what extent they should feel committed to the immediate impression. Pissarro was coming round to the view that the unity which the human spirit gives to vision can only be found in the studio. "It is there that our impressions – previously scattered – are coordinated, and give each other their reciprocal value, in order to create the true poem of the countryside."

Cézanne associated himself with Impressionism during its great decade, the 1870s, but it was an uneasy alliance. He was not happy with a painting being so dependent on the light of a specific moment of the day. He was not temperamentally suited to making rapid statements, which the outdoor technique demanded. Although he liked his subject in front of him as he painted and he used the bright palette of the Impressionists, he wanted to build forms with colour without being committed to particular effects of light. While Cézanne wholeheartedly endorsed the need to look at nature afresh, he was also drawn to the grand formal compositions of Poussin and stated that he wanted to paint similar works, but directly from nature.

Cézanne's early work was not greatly appreciated by his fellow artists, still less by the public. He decided to return to his native Provence where with the help of family money he was able to settle down to many years of single-minded industry. One advantage of this move was the more settled climate of the south. It is said that he sometimes deliberated for up to 20 minutes in between brush strokes; certainly he spent a month on some paintings.

A lesson from Cézanne's Impressionist days was that where there is colour at all, the whole scale is called into existence; where he might use blue to give the effect of recession, there is also a complementary orange to reaffirm the surface. His important achievement was to present a complete world where objects are seen as form in space, as a two-dimensional pattern and in terms of colour harmony. The colour harmony helps to achieve both form and pattern in such a way that each augments the other. His method was akin to that of a sculptor carving a relief – always being aware of the surface and yet conjuring up immense spaces from a relatively shallow incision. Cézanne's chisel was clean cool colour.

Cézanne declared a preference amongst painters of the past for the great colourists: Titian (c. 1487-1576), Tintoretto (1518-94), Veronese (1528-88) and Rubens, and his early work had an almost baroque character. Later, he used his powers to intellectualize the art of painting. He moved away from the naturalism of Constable, Pissarro and Monet, giving less importance to the purely visual function of the eye. "Monet is only an eye," he said (adding, "But what an eye!"). He gave form a greater identity than the atmospheric approach of Impressionism allowed, unwittingly following Piero della Francesca with his use of local colour and simple continuous outlines, minimizing shadows and reflected colour, applying paint thinly, not imitating textures with either brush or pigment, but letting colour determine texture. Impressionism could so easily degenerate into a mere copying of nature. Cézanne reinstated classical struc-

ture, with a tension of composition which had begun to disappear. He wanted us to see with the inner, not the physiological eye.

By the end of the century Cézanne was a lonely and suspicious man, almost a recluse, although he travelled to Paris regularly. In 1895, Pissarro suggested to Monet and Renoir that they encourage the young dealer Vollard to see what their friend from earlier days had been doing. The result was an exhibition of over 100 of Cézanne's paintings; Cézanne's friends, Degas included, bought as much as they could afford. He died in 1906 amidst a growing interest in his work but after the years of isolated innovation, he never believed his paintings were properly understood.

While Cézanne was working in Provence, Impressionism was being developed in a parallel but different way by Georges Seurat (1859-1891), a painter who saw himself more as scientist. The Impressionists had already broken their painted surfaces down into the colours of the spectrum, and had maintained that black did not exist in nature. Seurat took this idea further by using only the three primary colours, mixed with nothing but white. In his experiments with optical mixtures and colour theory he applied the primaries as hundreds of little dots over the surface of the canvas (popularly called Pointillism, but he preferred the term Divisionism). A green shape, for example, would be made up of yellow and blue dots. He also took a great interest in geometry and the Golden Section, and admired Piero della Francesca. Naturally, working as he did, his large paintings had to be executed in the studio. Like Cézanne, Seurat achieved great monumentality without sacrificing any of the new luminosity in painting gained by the Impressionists.

The bolder use of colour during the second half of

Above *La Montagne Sainte-Victoire* (1905), Paul Cézanne. This is a later version of the many paintings Cézanne made of this mountain. By taking some of the colours from the foreground and using them in the sky Cézanne was trying to make us aware of the flat surface of the canvas. Although the sky and the mountain are painted strongly, there is no doubt about the recession across the ground away from the spectator to the base of the mountain. Every tiny part of the canvas is treated with great intensity.

the nineteenth century had been almost universally welcomed by artists, but Cézanne and Seurat were not alone in wanting to achieve more than a purely visual representation of nature. Paul Gauguin (1848-1903), Vincent van Gogh (1853-1890) and Henri Matisse (1859-1954), were all important as generators of different non-naturalistic schools of painting in the twentieth century. To a greater or lesser extent, they all joined in the increasing interest in artistic traditions and cultures outside Western civilization: Islamic, Moorish, Oriental and primitive.

Gauguin rejected European ideas in general, and naturalistic representation in particular, countering Seurat's Divisionism with a style known as Synthetism. This involved the use of large areas of flat, strong colour which were juxtaposed to evoke moods and emotions – a source of much abstract art today.

Van Gogh's eventual difficulty with the Impressionist idiom, and consequent essays in both Seurat's and Gauguin's styles, was more closely connected with his own temperament than with any theorizing. As is well known, he led a life increasingly interrupted by periods of insanity, culminating in suicide, but not without moments of joy, as on his first discovery of the south of France. His problem as a painter was that he had learnt from the Impressionists and Seurat how to express delight, but not despair. Later he felt a need to say more about his own personal sensibilities and developed an agitated brushwork to animate his subjects. He made calculated distortions in perspective for particular purposes; an isolated figure on a road, which disappears into the distance with an exaggerated perspective, expresses loneliness and alienation. He also used simplified outlines and strong colour for emotional effect. Van Gogh and Gauguin were the prime influence on the Norwegian Edvard Munch (1863-1944) and a subsequent school of Expressionist painting.

Below *The Breakaway* (1891), Tom Roberts. Born in England, Tom Roberts went to Australia at the age of 13, but later returned to London to study. The almost photographic realism in this picture, imported from Victorian England, is employed to express the artist's excitement at the brightness of the light. It was this strong light that determined the characteristic blue and gold palette of subsequent schools of Australian landscape painters.

Above *Landscape at Collioure* (1906), Matisse. Although Matisse tried for a short while to make his colour schemes conform to the theories of some of his Post-Impressionist contemporaries, his exuberant approach expressed itself more easily by intuition. The freedom with which he applied colour to the canvas is deceptive; he composed his pictures with great care.

Centre right *Drouth Stricken Area* (1934), Alexander Hogue. This landscape is composed almost entirely of hard lines and angles, used to suggest the disappointments experienced by many pioneer farmers during the American Depression. The cow's ribs, echoed by the broken machine and the dry, ribbed sand, are the focus of the desolate isolation of the scene.

Above *Waterlilies* (1916-22), Claude Monet. This painting also hovers on the verge of abstraction, but within a different tradition. The many pictures of waterlilies made by Monet in his last years are often hailed as one of the starting points of abstract art, particularly Abstract Expressionism, but it would be more accurate to see them as a logical development of Monet's commitment to total naturalism and to recording the eye's sensations.

Right *Primrose Hill*, (1961), Frank Auerbach. Auerbach is a painter who uses colour as a tool for drawing the forms of the landscape, but never in a descriptive or naturalistic way. The result is a strong feeling of physical presence. The thickness of the paint is not the result of any interest in surface texture.

In 1905, a questionnaire devised by a journalist was sent to a large number of painters in France, asking for their views on trends in painting at the time. It was generally agreed that the freedoms gained by Impressionism had been of lasting value, but that greater content was sought. Gauguin and Cézanne were praised, the one for his rich and decorative colour, the other for his use of colour to create space and structure. Some answers to the questionnaire also suggested that artists should put more of their own personality into their work. Whatever measure of agreement was reached in their answers, artists at that time were working in a greater variety of directions than ever before, and have continued to do so.

At the turn of the century, the painter who emerged as the most able to assimilate these diverse forces was Henri Matisse. Never associating himself with any particular school, Matisse responded to many in a personal way, learning from Gauguin, Seurat and Cézanne, and from different cultures throughout the world. Matisse was able to combine decoration and structure in a unique way and his pictures, however free they seem at first glance, were always composed with rigorous care. In 1944 he gave an explanation of his approach: "The vertical is present in my mind; it helps me to define the direction of the other lines. . . I never draw a curve, for example a branch in a landscape, without bearing in mind its relation to the vertical." By implication, drawing and composition, the placing of shapes in relation to the edges of the paper or canvas, were inseparable. Nothing should be drawn without reference to its part in the whole.

Matisse's lifetime covered a period which saw not only rapid changes in the way artists treated their subjects, but also the disappearance of the subject altogether. Although the development of abstract art does not fall within the scope of this book, it is interesting to note that there have been many

Above *Trees and Barns* (1917), Charles Demuth (1833-1939). Demuth was an American artist who studied in Paris, and the influence of both Cézanne and the Cubists is manifest in this taut, elegant composition. The geometric shapes of the barns are used to intensify the organic twisting forms of the branches.

painters, such as Nicholas de Staël (1914-1955), who have taken landscape as a starting point for abstract painting. Other artists have reacted against abstraction, some by looking back to Cézanne, others by responding to the type of realism expressed by photographs.

Today, our knowledge and understanding of foreign traditions brings home the power that artists have always exerted over our manner of looking at nature. Travellers to China, who are familiar with

Left *Farm at Duivendrecht* (1907) Piet Mondrian (1872-1944). There is always some fascination in seeing the early work of an artist who has subsequently become associated with a particular style. Mondrian's later work is uncompromisingly abstract, mostly based on a black grid filled in with rectangles of colour. This early work, a romantic and stylized landscape, shows how radical a change he made

Chinese paintings, inevitably see the landscape through the eyes of its interpreters whereas, for the first painters who went from Europe to Australia where there was no tradition of landscape painting, it took a long time before they stopped seeing a European landscape in the Australian bush. We can now look back with amusement on those romantic poets, who were so conditioned by a tradition of landscape painting that they used a piece of tinted glass to force the English countryside to conform to their vision of a pastoral paradise.

This has only been a brief survey of the history of landscape painting in Western art. It would have been possible, especially for the earlier centuries, to write an alternative account, using quite different paintings .as examples. The artists discussed here have been chosen not only for the interest and beauty of their work, but also for their individual contributions to the development of landscape as a subject and their influence on other artists.

Representing Nature

Painting from nature is almost invariably the result of an artist combining many images and impressions collected over a length of time; it is a synthesis of his visual experiences. However, when the painter represents a varied collection of three-dimensional forms in space on the flat surface of his canvas he cannot avoid distorting what he has seen. Perspective is one convention which he can decide to employ in order to form these many images into a coherent entity; it is one method used to create pictorial space on a flat surface. Perspective has its own laws, but these are not laws of painting as a whole, and many artists choose not to use them. To choose to use them involves understanding the idea of a picture plane.

Using perspective

The picture plane Imagine holding up an empty picture frame or a sheet of glass squarely between you and the scene you are painting. It must be at right-angles to your line of vision and stay in the same position because it establishes a particular viewpoint in relation to the motif. If this viewpoint is altered during the course of the painting, it leads to inconsistencies in perspective.

To explain the reason for this, imagine sitting in the middle of a ploughed field. If you look at the field in one direction, the lines of the furrows will cross horizontally from one side to the other. If you make a right-angled turn, these lines will be going away towards the horizon. If you look to a corner of the field, they will be rising diagonally towards a point out of sight. If you decide to extend your line of vision and include the landscape beyond the ploughed field, looking directly across the furrows you will have horizontal lines across the foreground. If you want to include a wide vista, which involves looking from one side to another, consider what would happen to these horizontal furrows if you are altering the position of the picture plane. Looking through the imaginary picture frame towards a clump of trees at the right-hand corner of the field, the furrows would appear to fall away to the left; then, swinging the frame round towards the lefthand corner, the furrows would fall away to the right. To do the same for all the in-

Right *The Avenue at Middelharnis (1689),* Meindert Hobbema (1638-1709). Hobbema was a pupil of Ruisdael, and many of his works are very similar in style to those of his master. This one, however, has a quiet, peaceful atmosphere, whereas Ruisdael's often hint at a certain conflict between man and nature. What the paintings of the two artists certainly have in common is the emphasis given to large skies. Hobbema gave up painting in his early 30s and spent the next 40 years of his life testing wine.

termediate points, and combine the views, would produce a gradual curve for the edge of the field. Assuming that the field is relatively flat, this is clearly a distortion; it is only by accepting a fixed position for the picture plane that the edge of the field can be represented as a straight line.

It is also useful to check the angles which lines observed in the landscape make with the verticals and horizontals formed by the edges of the frame, and therefore the painting. This can easily be done by holding a paintbrush first vertically and then horizontally, and gauging the angle of the observed line against it. There are few absolutely flat landscapes in nature, but if the painter makes use of the principle of the picture plane and then looks for the variations, he will be better equipped to make sense of the space he is representing in his composition.

The vanishing point The next important step is to establish the eye level. If you now turn 90 degrees you see furrows going away towards the horizon. The angle the furrows make against other furrows will

Above left *The Fall of Icarus*, Pieter Bruegel. Although Bruegel painted many scenes of Biblical stories and of folk customs, this is his only reference to classical mythology. His treatment of the theme shows his preoccupation with everyday life, and a sympathy for the farmers whose labours are unaffected by dramatic events.

Above *Crossing the Ganges*, Akbar. This Persian painting shows a tradition that is completely different from that found in Western art. Some recession is achieved by the overlapping of forms, even though the most imposing figure, furthest away from us, is larger than the others. The decorative value of the figures, animals and the water clearly takes

precedence over an attempt at the spatial organization which is so important in Western art.

change according to your own height from the ground. When standing, your imaginary eye-level line will be the same distance from the ground as your eyes; if you can discern another person on the horizon you will know exactly where it is. The parallel furrows, if extended to the horizon, will appear to meet at a point on this level, which is called the vanishing point.

This point can be within the picture or outside it, depending on whether the furrows are parallel to your line of vision. If you are looking diagonally across the furrows to the corner of the field, they will have a vanishing point off the edge of the picture, but it will always be somewhere along the eye level.

If there is a hollow in the field, lines will converge below the eye level where they dip downwards and above it where they rise up again, although the vanishing point will stay on the same vertical axis. In this situation, most artists prefer to trust their own powers of observation rather than attempt to follow mathematical rules, but it is always important to keep the original picture plane and eye level in mind.

Linear perspective Perspective operates in all dimensions. An avenue of trees, for example, will recede according to the same laws. If the trees are planted in a straight line and are the same height, both the bases and the tops of the trees will form lines which will converge at the same point. *The Avenue at Middelharnis* by Hobbema (1638-1709), which shows a view of a a country lane running through an avenue of trees, where the vanishing point is at the level of the painter's eye above the ground in the middle of the lane, is a fine illustration of this. It does not, however, look like a picture from a textbook on perspective, because the artist has carefully observed all the variations that occur in nature. The trees are all different, the spaces between them are irregular, and the strong verticals which they make are offset by the horizontal accent of the lane turning away to the right, by the angles of the farm buildings and by the interest in the figures.

The angles that walls of buildings make with the picture plane is also important. If Hobbema's lines of of trees had rows of houses behind them, the sides of the houses looking onto the road would be at right-angles to the picture plane, and their bases and tops would therefore conform to the same vanishing point as the trees. If, on the other hand, you were looking straight onto a wall of a building, a square church tower for example, this wall would be parallel to the picture plane, its base and top horizontal, and its sides vertical. If you were very close to this wall and wanted to express its height, its sides would appear to converge on a vanishing point, even though they are built vertically from the ground. (The depth of a large hole could be expressed by the same means.) If the walls of the church tower were seen neither frontally nor at right-angles to the picture plane, they would have vanishing points at different points on the eye level. Natural phenomena, such as clouds, can also be seen to conform to the laws of perspective.

Atmospheric perspective Another spatial dimension is added by the use of tone and colour. All colours are

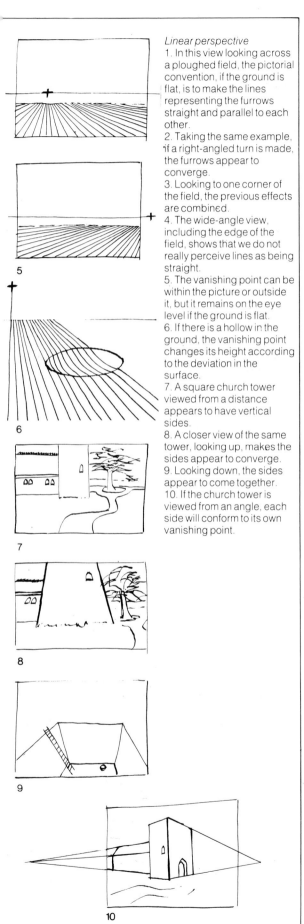

Linear perspective
1. In this view looking across a ploughed field, the pictorial convention, if the ground is flat, is to make the lines representing the furrows straight and parallel to each other.
2. Taking the same example, if a right-angled turn is made, the furrows appear to converge.
3. Looking to one corner of the field, the previous effects are combined.
4. The wide-angle view, including the edge of the field, shows that we do not really perceive lines as being straight.
5. The vanishing point can be within the picture or outside it, but it remains on the eye level if the ground is flat.
6. If there is a hollow in the ground, the vanishing point changes its height according to the deviation in the surface.
7. A square church tower viewed from a distance appears to have vertical sides.
8. A closer view of the same tower, looking up, makes the sides appear to converge.
9. Looking down, the sides appear to come together.
10. If the church tower is viewed from an angle, each side will conform to its own vanishing point.

Above and right Two views of Venice by Antonio Canaletto: *North East Corner of Piazza San Marco (above)* and *View of Piazza San Marco, Facing the Basilica (right)*. Canaletto embraced wholeheartedly the perspective systems pioneered earlier in Italy by Alberti, Uccello and Piero della Francesa. He was a highly skilled draughtsman but appreciated the value of the *camera obscura* as an aid to the drawing of complicated architectural detail. The *camera obscura* was a device which projected an upside-down reflection of a scene onto thin paper or glass, which could then be traced by the artist. Canaletto would have seen it as a useful time-saving gadget; he made hundreds of drawings and paintings of Venetian scenes which he sold to travellers on the Grand Tour.

observed through the atmosphere, which will affect our perception of them in accordance with their distance from the eye. For example, there will be more blue in a green field which is further away.

A tree trunk which has sunlight playing on one side will have a dark side where the sun does not strike it. The greater the distance from which it is viewed, the less the contrast between the lighter and darker side. From a distance the darker side seems to become lighter because the atmosphere is itself illuminated; the shadow on the tree trunk will seem progressively lighter the further it is away. The lighter side will become very slightly darker according to the density of atmosphere, but to a lesser extent than the shadow gets lighter.

In paintings, strong contrasts of tone or colour make objects appear closer. It is important for a painter to be able to compare the tonal values in what he sees. A good exercise is to compare objects of different colour and try to discern which is lighter or darker in tone than the other. In composing a painting it often helps to pick out the lightest and the darkest tones in the scene, and place everything in its appropriate place within this tonal scale. Experience will dictate how closely to stick to these literal observations when it comes to mixing colours and actually putting them on the canvas.

The accurate observation of tonal values is an important skill to develop and is closely linked with observation of colour. In terms of aerial perspective, colours are also subject to enormous variation according to prevailing conditions of light and atmosphere, and, as a general rule, they become less intense at a distance. There are lesser contrasts of colours in the more humid atmospheric conditions of northern Europe than in the drier climates of the Mediterranean or parts of Australia. This partly explains the greater concern with aerial perspective shown by Dutch, English, and northern French painters such as the Impressionists.

If the aim of the painter is to create space on a flat surface, it might seem a simple matter to make things recede by making them bluer and paler, but, as with linear perspective, each separate picture has its own compositional demands. Distance is not the same thing as pictorial space, which only comes to life where there is an interplay or a tension between space and the flat pattern of the picture's surface.

Composition

It is not possible to separate an artist's use of either aerial or linear perspective from the way he approaches composition as a whole. If it is accepted that a picture aims to create its own world, then the eye of the spectator must be guided to read it as such. If a landscape painting depicts a large vista, the spectator's eye must be led around it from one point to another, in such a way that the painting can be understood as a complete entity. This constitutes movement in a painting. The painting is static; "movement" refers to the way in which the eye of the spectator is guided by the points of emphasis.

There are no rules about what makes a good composition because there are so many variables: colour, tone, intensity of colour, strength of lines, paint texture, quality of brushstrokes, and so on. Nevertheless, there have been many theories on the subject. One school of thought maintained that the painter should imagine an oval within the rectangle of the canvas and ensure nothing important was placed

Below *The Battle of San Romano*, Paolo Uccello. This is one of the earliest paintings where pictorial space is expressed by linear perspective. The foreshortened figure of the dead soldier and some of the broken lances have fallen most conveniently to the ground at right-angles to the picture plane.
Right *The Pond* L.S. Lowry. This artist, along with many twentieth century painters, has evolved his own personal approach to perspective. In this case, the aerial view distances the spectator from the scene and enables him to embrace a wide panorama. There is no real focal point which would lead us to any centre of activity.

 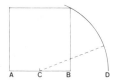 

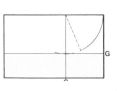

The Golden Section
This proportional system is based on canons of geometric proportion employed by the architects of ancient Greece, but to use a canvas of this shape does not unfortunately guarantee a good composition. The measurement of the smaller side of the canvas is decided, and the longer side is then obtained by geometry, as above. The final rectangle contains a square and another rectangle which is the same proportion as the larger one.

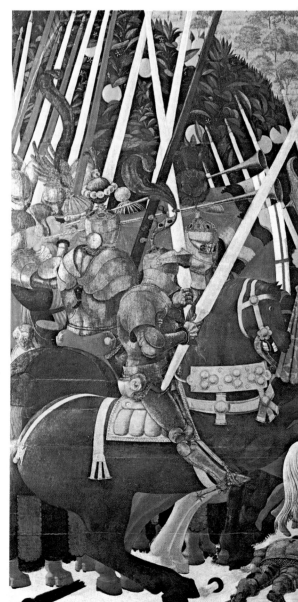

Above *Jetty*, J.M.W. Turner. This chalk drawing is from Turner's sketchbook, and shows the artist's intuitive approach to drawing. The proportions of the figures compared with the jetty and boats are not necessarily accurate in terms of classical perspective. This was not Turner's concern; he was far more interested in the conditions of light, here achieved with the use of light chalk on a dark paper.

outside this oval – that is, near the corners of the picture. Entire books have also been written about using the Golden Section. This refers to a method of placing shapes on the canvas in a way which divides the canvas into satisfying proportions. First, the canvas itself must be of certain dimensions. If these dimensions are progressively subdivided in the same way, the canvas will always contain a square, and another rectangle the same proportion as the original.

There is no harm in such theories if the painter has an interest in them; the mistake lies in giving them overwhelming importance. Many artists have made elaborate use of the Golden Section, notably Piero della Francesca, Nicolas Poussin and Georges Seurat, but these artists understood what they were doing and why. Certainly, the geometry in Piero's work contributes greatly to the whole, but apart from being a painter he was also a distinguished mathematician. If such systems do not hold a particular fascination for the artist they are best left.

In practice, many paintings contain divisions

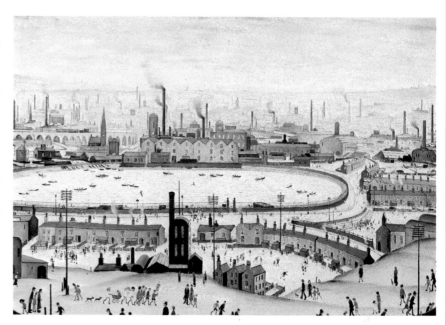

without conscious intention on the part of the artist, and it is better to compose by intuition than risk stultifying personal responses to nature by conforming to a prescribed method. There are ways of placing things on the canvas that an experienced artist might avoid, but it is dangerous to generalize. However, there can be some guide as to what to avoid. For example, a very emphatic line or division across a picture, without any links of colour or direction from one side of the line to the other, is likely to divide the work into two. Emphatic continuous lines retain the eyes' attention, and unless they take the spectator on a three-dimensional tour of the space, the picture will appear flat. Similarly, a strong line around a delicately modelled form will take the eye away from the subtleties of the modelling.

Rather than trying to memorize a list of generalized rules about what not to do, it is better to understand the principles which inform these rules. The artist attempts to guide the spectator into experiencing the same emotions that he felt on looking at the forms in nature, and to share the excitement of translating them onto a flat surface. It is the tension between the potential effects of lines and colours on this surface and the three-dimensional forms that they represent, which results in an understanding of space. If the artist directs our attention to the brow of a hill in the distance, for example, by leading us to a point on the surface of the canvas, he must also consider where he will direct our attention next. The landscape painter sitting in a field can choose to concentrate on whichever part of the view he wants, but the eye which looks at his painting of this view expects to be guided by the marks the painter has made, and not to be stranded. It is a spatial journey.

Many paintings contain a centre of interest or focal point, but this need not be placed centrally; the lines or masses which lead the eye towards it will determine its position. It is possible to overplay the importance of what might seem the most interesting part of the scene at the beginning of a painting. For example, the painter might find his eye continually drawn to an enticing vista of parkland glimpsed through a gate. Perhaps the grass through the gate is illuminated by the sun more brightly than the surrounding vegetation, and his eye is drawn to this stronger contrast. The painter must try to understand why this part of the landscape is of particular interest. If he were to paint this section in close-up, he might find that he was destroying the particular elements which first gave it a fascination. It could be much more effective to place the view through the gate in its longer setting, not too obviously in the middle of the canvas, so that the spectator discovers it just as the painter had. Having found it, the spectator might be led away by another accent, subsequently to return.

Using a window cut out of cardboard can aid the artist in selecting a composition. The inside measurements of the window should be in the same proportions as the canvas or paper you intend to use. Hold the window out at arm's length to see how much sky or foreground you wish to include. Turn the window around to see whether the scene might be better treated in a vertical format.

Left *Farm Outhouse* In this pen and ink drawing, strong areas of dark tone make a frame for the real centre of attention, the farm building. Fine descriptive drawing is balanced with the heavier patches of shadow and foliage. Because of the nature of the pen marks, the dark tones are enlivened by small areas of white. By exploiting the variety of marks possible with pen and ink, the artist has created a range of tones which not only provide greater depth and interest, but also are the means for creating balance and harmony in the composition.
Below left *Summer in Ireland (1863)*, Seymour Haden (1818-1910). During the nineteenth century, printmaking in England suffered from a certain lack of creative force. Haden was instrumental in effecting a revival. Together with Whistler and Alphonse Legros (1837-1911), he founded the Society of Painter-Etchers, of which he was the first president. He made an intense study of Rembrandt's etchings but also anticipated in some measure the revolutionary work of the Impressionists. He brought a freshness and vitality to the art of etching.

Early decisions

It is at the beginning of a work that the artist should most closely examine the motives and reasons for being drawn to a particular scene. Is it the colour of the shadows? Is it a particular shape in the hills, which might be as well expressed, for example, by charcoal or some other medium? Even when time is limited, a few minutes' contemplation can be valuable.

The first decision to be taken, when starting a picture directly from nature, concerns the time available for its completion. An artist often sees something he wants to paint when he has neither the time nor the equipment. He must then decide whether a quick drawing, and perhaps a photograph, will give him sufficient information to be able to treat the scene as he would wish.

If the movement of the sun is going to alter the appearance of the scene or the artist's ideas about it, this will affect the way in which he or she should approach the picture. If the light conditions are of

Above *Salisbury Cathedral*, John Constable. Constable used here a compositional device which creates, to some extent, a picture within a picture. The cathedral is set in space by positioning it so we see it through the frame of trees in the foreground. Constable has also used the old leaning trees to offset the gothic perpendiculars of the architecture.

Right A common way of enlarging a sketch or preparatory drawing for a painting is to rule a fine grid of lines over the drawing and then do the same on a larger scale on the canvas. If this method is to be of any real value, the grid must be drawn accurately, because small errors of measurement on the drawing will be magnified.

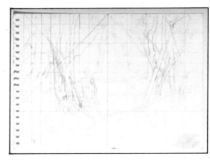

Right *Pines Near the Mediterranean* This shows a vigorous use of pastel which expresses the character and rhythm of the pine trees with swiftly executed strokes of colour. The trunks at either side are dark, placed so as to frame the glimpse of bright blue sea and sky beyond, with the pinks and pale yellows of the middle distance contrasting with the dark blue-greens of the trees' shadows. These colours give us a strong feeling of heat.

vital interest, it may be best to make detailed statements on the canvas about the colours, possibly with some working drawings and notes in a sketchbook, and complete the work at home.

Monet, who was interested in the effects of light above all else, seldom worked on the same picture for more than two hours at a time in a day. Within two hours, colour values can change considerably. The ideal arrangement for a painting of any size is to work for a short period over several days, or weeks if necessary. If this is not possible the size of the picture must be considered accordingly.

Artists have different feelings about the extent to which they need the subject in front of them as they paint. For some, it is essential all the time, the direct visual response being painting's prime concern. If there is limited time, the picture may then have to be small. For other artists, possibly endowed with good visual memories, colour notes supported by a drawing are sufficient to sustain even a large work away from the subject. The only way to find out what is individually appropriate is to try both. It is a good thing anyway to complete an occasional painting on the spot, with nothing invented or guessed at, even if it is tiny and the forms simplified.

Having decided on the size, the shape might also seem a problem to the inexperienced, and experienced artists occasionally change their minds about this even when the work is under way. In practice it is not a critical choice. If it is not excessively long and narrow, one of the challenges of the painting will be to make the composition work within the available rectangle, although to an experienced eye there will be subjects which appear to demand particular proportions. The shape of canvases are often referred to as either "landscape" or "portrait", which means no more than that the painting is either horizontal or vertical. A landscape can be painted on a "portrait" canvas and vice versa. A sensible beginning could be a canvas of about 18 x 24 inches (45 x 60 cm), or smaller or larger in the same proportion. (The vertical measurement of a picture is always given first.) The time available and the medium chosen will influence the actual size.

Left *Hillside in Shadow* This landscape is executed on a portrait-shaped canvas. The composition is given stability by the roof in the foreground, which also contrasts manmade shapes with the trees on the slopes behind. The artist has been attracted by the clarity of the lit parts of the landscape and their almost total disappearance into the mysterious shadow above.

Preparatory sketches

Preparatory, even small and sketchy drawings are always helpful because they stimulate the act of objective observation and help to sort out the feel of the composition, its stronger accents and the placing of lines and masses. Some artists choose to do this on the canvas itself, and others feel more confident making an initial pencil drawing on paper. If there is a desire to keep the eventual colours as bright and transparent as possible, the less overpainting on canvas the better.

As an aid to this planning, you can make a window out of a small piece of card or stiff paper, through which the basic proportions of the landscape can be assessed in relation to the proportions of the canvas. The outside measurements of the card are of no account. In the middle of the card, cut a hole of the same proportions as the canvas. This window can then be held at a distance from the eye so that the features across the landscape that you wish to include are visible, and you will be able to see how much of the foreground or sky will fit into that proportion. Conversely, if you definitely want to include certain features in the foreground at the bottom of the canvas and a certain amount of sky above the horizon at the top, you will be able to see how much will fit on either side, and you may decide as a result of this experiment to turn the canvas round, so that the vertical side is the longer. A refinement is to tape two bits of thread vertically and horizontally across the exact middle of the window so that the central point of the view can be established. This will facilitate the subsequent judgement of distances and their placing on the canvas. If such devices are to be used, they must be made accurately and held squarely before the eye, as the window represents the "picture plane"; otherwise they are useless.

In the familiar image of the artist at work, he is not using his pencil for drawing, but holding it up in front of a screwed-up eye and measuring a length on it with his thumbnail. This is another way of calculating intervals. The horizontal distance between trees, for example, can be measured off by the eye along the length of the pencil, or any straight edge, and then compared with the height of a tree by turning the pencil upright. But, if this method is not used

Right A wide variety of sketchbooks are available, ranging in size from small pocket types to larger ones more suitable for detailed work. Sketchbooks also come either in portrait (upright) or landscape (oblong) formats. Some have spiral bindings or perforated pages; others are bound in book form so it is possible to work across two pages. Sketchbooks can be improvised – from blank diaries as in the example shown here – or made up to the artist's specifications. The medium chosen for sketching depends very much on personal preference, but it is important to remember that charcoal and pastel will smudge without fixing.

Sketches
This selection of sketches shows the diversity of approaches – from simple notes on form and composition to full detailed drawings. In the sketch of a hillside with houses *(above)*, the artist has roughed out a suggestion of shapes in pencil. In contrast, the pen and ink drawing of a Berkshire farm *(centre)* is a complete work in its own right. The drawing has been reinforced with ink washes, strengthening the trees and adding to the forms of the buildings by selectively applying tone. White gouache was added in places. The detailed drawing of the old tin mine *(above right)* is an example of the sort of work which is best carried out in a fairly large bound sketchbook, so the drawing can be carried across two pages. The information such drawings provide is excellent reference for later work in the studio. The rapid but strong pencil drawing of the aqueduct *(below right)* was also made in a sketchbook. The forms of the trees have been expressed by the shapes of the shaded areas, the artist having selected what would give a sense of strong light. The aqueduct, seen against the light, with the diminishing perspective of its arches, has given the artist the opportunity to encompass a large expanse of space.

care, the results will be inaccurate. First, the pencil must be held at exactly the same distance from the eye all the time; errors here are greatly magnified over the larger distances of the landscape. Second, it must be held still. Third, any position of the pencil must be at right-angles to the line of vision because it is representing the imaginary surface of the picture plane. There are painters who are particularly interested in the mechanics of vision inherent in this approach, and for greater accuracy would use a plumb line to be sure of having a true vertical. The inexperienced should start by training the eye to judge true distances before being committed to only one of many ways of looking at and representing the world.

Representing light and colour
Whether mathematics or intuition have been employed in the planning of the composition, no one element in painting can be isolated from the others, and there are immediately other factors to be taken into account. Light, strong or subdued, should immediately be influencing the marks made on the canvas. In a strong light, the composition should not

Right This example demonstrates how to achieve combinations of colour and tone by identifying the range of colours and building up an overall effect with small dabs of colour. This type of pointillist approach is very effective from the point of view of paint surface, but is not a means of precise representation. It is possible to float colours into each other, by adjusting the proportions of one colour to another in different parts of the painting, but this is not effective if the colours are not allowed to mix freely or if one colour or group becomes isolated or overbalanced.

Below right *An Afternoon at La Grande Jatte*, Georges Seurat. Seurat brought a scientific approach to his perception of colour, from which he evolved a method which he called "divisionism". The shadows are made up of colours which are complementary to the colours in the adjacent areas of light. For example, where the local colour of grass is made up of green and yellow, the nearby shadow will contain red and blue. The timeless, static quality of his paintings is a result of his interest in compositional theories derived from the use of the Golden Section.

Above right *Dido Building Carthage* (detail), J.M.W. Turner. In his early years, Turner painted nothing but watercolours, and when he started using oils he made much use of the glazing techniques employed by watercolourists. In this painting, the luminosity of the sky is achieved in this way. Turner was a great admirer of Claude, who had painted skies at all times of the day. This painting anticipates Turner's later preoccupation with skies.

Far right *Waterlilies: Harmony in Green*, Claude Monet. Painted in the ornamental garden which Monet created for himself towards the end of his life, this is just one of many paintings on the theme of waterlilies. He often worked on several different pictures during the same day, leaving one aside as the light changed.

probably be based on the topographical layout of the landscape because the strength of contrasts created by the sun and the shapes and colours of shadows may well create a pattern demanding a particular placing on the flat surface. Many artists start by blocking in the main dark areas, for the pattern of light and dark is what gives a picture its initial impact, and it is a good idea to start seeing the work in terms of shapes from an early stage. The only disadvantage of this is that the dark colours used to represent these dark masses could be too much of a generalization. On the other hand, a too-detailed linear drawing on the canvas, however accurate as a drawing, can obstruct the observations which will express a sense of light, observations which are often of very subtle changes in colour and tone.

The painter, excited by a visual idea, is faced with the problem of getting it onto canvas as quickly as possible, whether that means three hours or three months. He wants the picture to be complete as soon as it is started. For this reason he should try to keep the work complete from the first moment, so that, in a sense it is finished at any stage, whether it is just a note about colour relationships or a much fuller statement about forms in space. Of course, changes will be

made as the picture develops; it may start as just a few patches of colour and then grow into something much more detailed and complex. But these early patches of colour can and should have a unity because they have been observed in relationship to each other. It is of limited value to put only one colour onto the canvas. The patches will probably be no more than an abstraction of the colours seen in a particular place at a particular time, but they will have a significance.

As far as possible, it is best to avoid putting anything on the canvas which will obviously need subsequent alteration but there are many different ways in which the same subject can be painted and deferring a decision will probably only multiply the problems of selection. Suggestions of colours should be introduced at the earliest possible stage, giving an idea of their potential impact.

No two people perceive colour in exactly the same way. Also, it is impossible to see one colour on its own, and its translation into paint will lead to further differences of interpretation. This is leaving aside any degree of colour blindness that might affect an individual. It may be generally agreed that a particular barn door is brown, but this "brown-ness" cannot be conveyed on the canvas with any accuracy without

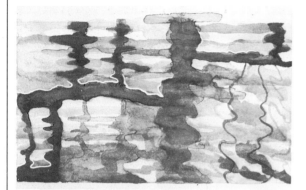

putting it into the context of the surrounding colours. If the barn walls are made of a warm-coloured brick, the door may appear a cool brown; if they are made of grey stones it may appear warmer, and so on. And both door and walls will be seen in the context of the whole landscape – the blue of the sky, the green of the fields or whatever surrounds them. There are no absolutes in colour, only relationships.

This brown will be altered again by conditions of light and atmosphere. The actual brown of the wood it is made of, or the colour it is painted, is its "local" colour. This local colour will be modified: if the sun strikes it, it will become warmer; if it is in shadow it will become cooler because it is influenced by the blue of the sky. Imagine the whole barn, built of grey stones, illuminated by the sun on one wall, with the wall where the door is in shadow. The three-dimensional aspect of the barn can be expressed by the contrast between its lit and unlit sides, by warm and cool colour respectively. The brighter the light, the greater this contrast will be; the wall in shadow will lose its local colour increasingly in relation to the brightness of the other wall, and become submerged in the colours chosen to express the shaded areas.

As the eye is presented with such a variety of colours in nature, it might seem sensible when representing nature with paint to acquire as many different tubes or sticks of colour as are manufactured, in preparation for any conditions. In practice the reverse is true. To endow a picture with any degree of subtlety or richness it is essential to be able to mix colours, so that each hue can be rendered in its full range of tone and intensity. When familiar with minute tonal differences, an artist may notice that a

Above left These two watercolour studies illustrate the specific problems of reflection. The first is a purely graphic representation of patterns in water and is a combination of hard-edged shapes, linear qualities and fuzzy colour.

Colour in water depends on the surroundings. The second study is of a heavy rain cloud over water. As with water, clouds and sky cannot be studied enough. Although it is tempting to use photographs to freeze an effect, it is important to

capture the sense of movement and space, making frequent studies so the effects of colour, light and form can be fully understood. It is also important to achieve some transparency when painting skies. Wet paint applied to wet areas gives

particular picture demands the use of a certain green, for example, and if it cannot be made from the blue and yellow already available, only then may it be necessary to increase the range of pigments.

The painter now has to make a decision about how much he wants to express the feeling of light. The Impressionists, who had brightened the painter's palette and used strong colours for their shadows, tended to give precedence to the effects of light, letting the formal aspect of objects, their precise shape and local colour, take second place. The brown of the barn door will be affected, even lost, by being in the shade; similarly bright light will detract from the force and variety of local colours, rather than enhancing them as might be expected. There is a point where the door would lose its unique brown-ness altogether.

These two possible approaches to representing form in colour provoked Cézanne to ask, "To yield to the atmosphere or to resist it?" His own answer was: "To yield is to deny the 'localities', to resist is to give them their force and variety." He tended to give objects their local colour and pay less attention to atmospheric conditions.

Left This ink and watercolour wash drawing is a study of direct reflection – in this case of two trees. The reflected image should not be an exact mirror of the object, especially if there is movement in the water. If a more graphic approach is desired, it is possible to formalize general tendencies of reflected patterns, as David Hockney has done in his swimming pool paintings.
Far left *Dedham*, John Constable. Constable always made many studies on the spot, both simple and elaborate, and in a variety of media. This pen and wash drawing concentrates on the contrast of light and shade and includes nothing which is not relevant to this theme. The spontaneity of the brushstrokes contributes a lively directness which is characteristic of Constable's out-of-doors sketches.

fuzzy edges which are useful for showing thin clouds. Blotting with a tissue lifts colour so different tones can be achieved.

If there is no direct sunlight, the colour of the two walls of the barn will probably be much the same, their local colour more apparent. The painter may have to look hard to be able to represent different tones for the side and end walls to express the change of plane at the corner of the building. If he can see no difference, the expression of this right-angle may depend entirely on his observation of the angles of the roof. An error in drawing here might turn the form inside out. He might, however, find that one wall is slightly cooler than the other, because they will reflect what light there is in different ways being set at different angles. This raises an important aspect of colour which is of especial use to the painter – its temperature. It is difficult to think of a single painting where forms in space are successfully represented without making use of the interplay of warm and cool colours. Even where strong local colours are used, a sense of light cannot exist without this variation of temperature. Warm colours tend to come forward while cooler colours recede.

Having placed objects in coherent spatial relationships, a painter may want to say something about the material nature of these objects. It is a temptation which should probably be resisted until the more important problems of space, light and composition have been solved; some would argue that it should be resisted altogether. However, it cannot be denied that the quality of a surface conditions its observed colour, and objects reflect light according to the hardness of their surface; the surface cannot be entirely ignored. A black woollen garment will be very little affected by its surroundings, whereas a polished steel surface will be altered dramatically. In fact polished steel sometimes appears to have no local colour, its surface being nothing but reflections. This would present another situation where the artist must choose between representing the local colour of an object or the way the colour is modified by the environment. There may be a temptation to show the shiny surface of an apple by adding the tiny reflection of light coming in through a window, but if this is slightly overdone the three-dimensional form of the apple will be destroyed. At all stages, the painter is presented with a whole range of decisions which, if deferred, could lead to chaos.

Right This painting of a garden was worked entirely in gouache. The intention was to give an overall impression of light and colour. The spindly forms of the roses in the foreground help to give definition to the space.

Left This study of clouds was executed in pencil with a cobalt blue watercolour wash. Clouds are constantly changing; rapid studies over a period of time give the opportunity to practise rendering the effects of light and form.
Below This is a mixed media work in watercolour, pastel and gouache. The texture of the drawing is not really intended to represent movement but there was a vibrant effect of light in the orchard through the branches and blossom which the artist chose to render by using layers of paint washes and scribbled pastel marks. This is an impression of light and colour, not a portrait of the scene.

4

Colour studies: paint
These paint mixtures are a number of greys and browns obtained by mixing pairs of complementary colours. In each *(1, 2 and 3)* the vertical centre row is a mixture of equal parts of the complementaries: neat at the top and with white added in two proportions below and centre. On the left and right of each centre row are the effects of overbalancing towards one colour or another. To compare the types of grey, a simple black/white scale *(4)* is provided.

1

2

3

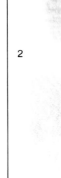

1

2

3

Colour studies: pencil
These studies show the range of tones possible by building up with overlapping layers of coloured pencil.
1. Basic green overlaid with bright green, brown, blue, yellow, red.
2. Yellow and green crosshatching overlaid with grainy shading in the same green.
3. Blue overlaid with brown, and green overlaid with brown.

Working indoors

So far the problems considered have been related to working directly from nature; given time and settled weather this is usually the most satisfactory, despite difficulties. It is important not to give up too easily, because the freshness gained in the painting can more than compensate for the problems encountered in achieving it. The advantages of having your subject before you are obvious, but anyone who has stood in a field with a large canvas on a windy day with horseflies and inquisitive children hovering and rainclouds on the horizon, will acknowledge the attractions of working at home.

Other reasons that may make it desirable to work away from the motif include the increased opportunity to plan the composition and the proportions of the

canvas, which can be much larger. Sketches and notes made in the field need to be extensive. A painting started on the spot may consist of just a few tentative strokes, which will give a basic planning of the flat surface, but a preparatory drawing can be made to explore precise spatial relationships. However accurate, it may not be sufficient if it is only linear. It should have a feeling for the strength of light and, the exact positions of shadows.

The best way of approaching such a drawing may be to consider what enables you to see objects as three-dimensional forms, and why you perceive the spatial relationships between them. For example, why do you observe a group of buildings in the distance as more than just a series of flat shapes? Is is because some of the buildings are receding in accord-

Above For this pencil and watercolour drawing of a headland, the artist used photographs of the same scene as reference. Several pictures were taken of the cliff from different angles; the photographs were then cropped and pasted together to give a composite picture, with a wider angle of view. The interest in this scene was the folded rocks and lines of vegetation; in making the drawing the artist chose to exaggerate this aspect by drawing the scene at low tide. Photographs are useful sources of information when a drawing cannot be made on the spot, but, as in this example, it is important to adapt the reference to your own requirements rather than simply copy what the camera has recorded.

Left *Trees and Undergrowth* This watercolour places us in the midst of a tangle of plants and branches. The artist has decided that what expresses this density is variety, of form and colour. A wide range of greens has been used together with transparent and opaque washes and a variety of colour mixtures has been explored. There is also observation of the individual character of different branches: straight and slender, heavy and bowed, light and spidery, all contributing to the general feeling of profusion.

Above In this cloud study a watercolour wash was combined with gouache. A thin wash of cobalt blue was applied and then wet white gouache was dropped in and allowed to spread. When using thick opaque paint to suggest heavier clouds, the tones will need to be adjusted and will often need to be lighter than appears at first.

ance with the laws of linear perspective? Or, if they are too far away to see tiny changes of direction, is it because the angle of light shows up the receding planes. If a band of trees appears as a flat shape, then an outline may be enough for the drawing, but a note about its colour will be needed to establish its position in space.

A painter develops his own language for making written notes about colour. To start with it may be plainly descriptive such as "very pale blue-green", but with experience of using a certain range of colours these descriptions may develop into references to particular pigments.

Photographs or colour transparencies can help with some details, but they have limitations. The camera's eye only records what it sees for a fraction of a second. It does not register an understanding of form, and cannot accumulate the experiences of looking over a period of time. There are also technical problems: only the experienced photographer knows exactly which film to put into the camera and which filters to use in any given condition of light, to approach accuracy of colour. On the whole, transparencies still give more reliable colour than prints, mostly because the processing is more direct, and they can be useful when, for one reason or another, it is impossible to make an adequate drawing. They can be projected onto a canvas to establish positions, but distortions are possible. The projector must be level and the canvas vertical; the canvas must be exactly at right-angles to the centre of the projected image. This can be checked by making sure the distances from each side of the canvas to the projector's lens are the same. In a darkened room, the image on the canvas can be lightly marked in, but this must not be confused with drawing. The camera cannot capture perspective according to our pictorial conventions so, where we might make the side of a building vertical, and parallel with the sides of the canvas, the camera will demonstrate the operation of linear perspective in every dimension, and the building will become narrower as it gets further away from the lens. The camera will also demonstrate that landscape is a section of a circular globe, and will not obligingly straighten lines which we have chosen to see straight for pictorial purposes. Sophisticated lenses devised to keep straight lines straight are, unfortunately, expensive.

It is important to understand that these distortions are taking place so that the photographic image is not taken too literally. Although a good transparency provides clues about tonal relationships and two-dimensional proportions, it cannot offer that unique perception of the physical relationship between the artist or the spectator and the world, which distinguishes a good painting.

We are aware at times of the physical strangeness of the world; this is the experience an artist seeks when he works. With what sense of wonder must a sixteenth-century Dutch painter, travelling to Italy from the flat landscapes of his homeland, have arrived in the Alps. More mundanely, you can provoke this sensation of extraordinariness by bending over and looking for a few moments at a strange, new world. The forms, the spatial intervals, the colours, all have a new, three-dimensional vividness. In the same way, when you wake in a strange room, ordinary objects in unfamiliar juxtaposition can acquire a new richness. The aim of the artist must be to represent this sensation, to recreate in his own individual way those spaces in nature which have moved him.

Far left *April Evening* A freely executed oil painting made from a much more precise watercolour study *(left)* which was painted on the spot. The study, while in itself a finished picture, contains enough important information to give the artist confidence to handle the paint vigorously and with freedom. There has been no attempt to copy the study in a literal way; even the proportions have been changed.

Left *Gates in Normandy* In contrast to the above painting, this was made from a transparency which the artist took himself, having felt sufficiently interested in the subject to make a painting, but not having any more time than it takes to focus a camera. The nature of the subject naturally demanded precise information, particularly as the sun was in a position where it just touched the top of the palm trees and the ridge of the roof.

Left *Venice Moonshine* Hercules Brabazon. A gouache study which has been made freely and rapidly, with solid colour laid over both wet and dry areas of wash. Despite the sketchiness of some parts, such as the reflections, the trees have been observed and established with considerable accuracy.
Far left This pair of studies show how local colour, that is, the actual colour of an object, can be dramatically altered by bright sunlight. The difference of warm and cool colours enables the painter to establish the solidity of the barn in the top study, but in the sunless conditions *(below)* where both visible walls are closer in colour, the end wall has been made cooler to express the change of plane.

Drawing

Almost everyone can make a great variety of marks on a piece of paper – when someone bemoans the fact that they "cannot draw" they really mean that they have not learnt how to observe. The quality of a drawing depends more on the artist's ability to observe, than on any special skill with pen or pencil. The ideal drawing medium for each artist is the one which expresses his observations most directly. When an artist chooses a medium to draw with, he looks for the one which will become an expressive extension of his fingers, so that his hand and eye can work together with as little impediment as possible. Naturally this choice will be influenced by the nature of his observations: it would be difficult to say much about a delicate cloud formation with a laundry marker.

The great advantage of an ordinary pencil, provided it is not too hard, is that the strength of the mark it makes is open to considerable variation, from light to heavy. Pen and ink may seem less flexible by comparison, but a pen drawing by a great master such as Rembrandt is a reminder that it is not so much the nature of marks made on the paper which is important, as the quality of the observation which has informed them.

Provided that it is used to express form, almost any drawing medium can come to life. It can be instructive to draw the same object using as many different materials as possible, in order to find out which one is most successful for conveying space and volume. If the object is drawn as an outline, using a medium which gives too even a line will make the drawing seem flat and formless. It would be more appropriate to draw the outline with a soft pencil or some other marker which has variable strengths and tones. If there are strong contrasts of light and shade in the object, with large dark areas, then charcoal might be the most suitable medium. It is important, however, to be aware of each medium's limitations; in fact, the

particular discipline imposed by any medium can act as a stimulus.

It is also important not to be influenced by colour when making a monochromatic drawing. Although colours contribute to the understanding of a form, we have to force ourselves to look for other signposts when drawing. Only where a colour change is also a change of plane will it interest the draughtsman; expressing a change of colour by shading may mistakenly indicate a change of plane. A sense of light, on the other hand, is important from the outset.

Drawings, normally made by dark marks on a pale, if not white, surface, depend on tonal variation and contrast, but to become exclusively preoccupied with light and shade can prevent artists from discovering the pencil's ability to make expressive lines, immediate responses to observation. It is often when the artist is working quickly that he produces his best drawings; when there is no time to be selfconscious about the nature of the marks he is making and his pencil becomes a part of his hand. Students in some art schools are encouraged to alternate long, thoughtful studies with very rapid ones to achieve a command of drawing. Eventually, quick two-minute sketches can be progressively prolonged to become fuller and more thorough drawings without losing the immediacy and expressiveness.

It is easy to start a drawing without thinking about how it will placed on the paper, but the spatial implications of this placing should not be ignored. Often the illusion of space is destroyed when an object is drawn in the middle of a large sheet of paper with no suggestion of surroundings. A drawing is, after all, often exploratory work for painting, and composition and drawing should be seen as inseparable. It is simple enough to pencil a frame around a drawing. If the frame is drawn in alternative positions, the effect it can have on our feelings for the subject, its dynamics and priorities will be obvious.

Right *Behind the Trees.* The artist has begun this drawing with an open mind as to which medium will best express feelings about the subject. Pencil and two coloured chalks have been used alternately to build up the image in a very free and direct manner. The wild tangle of the trees' branches have been simplified by the use of black and red chalk, with firmer statements in pencil where appropriate.

Left *A Path Bordered by Trees*, Peter Paul Rubens. Rubens is best known for his grand Baroque paintings, but it is always refreshing to have a glimpse of his more intimate studies. The handling of the trees is both free and delicate. It is undoubtedly only a study for a small part of a much larger composition, yet Rubens has achieved much more than a mere working drawing.

Centre left *Harbour on the Schelde*, Albrecht Dürer. This very fine line drawing is precise yet economical The solidity of the forms is realized with sparing touches. Each shape is related most carefully to all the others in such a way that the whole image acquires a unity which is more than a sum of parts. Dürer was the main transmitter of Italian Renaissance ideas to northern Europe.

Left *View of Wivenhoe Park*, John Constable. Constable demonstrates here how much can be achieved with the pencil alone. The forms of the landscape are firmly established in space, but also the quality and texture of each part is given due weight. The cornfield in the foreground has its own character defined with the simplest of means, and the delicate treatment of the sky is equally sensitive to light and texture.

Paper

Paper is all too often taken for granted, but it can discolour and even disintegrate; so it is sensible to have some understanding of how to look after it. As paper is made of organic material, it is sensitive to light, temperature, humidity and other atmospheric factors. A good sheet of paper can be very expensive, and artists who use a lot of high quality paper are advised to treat it with a great deal of care. The surface of a thin cheap paper might be preferred for some types of work, and will need even more care.

A combination of light and acidity is paper's main enemy. Both before and after use, paper should be stored wrapped in acid-free paper (not in polythene bags which would prevent it from breathing). Paper should also be kept in a room which is not subject to great changes in temperature or humidity. If paper is constantly absorbing moisture from the air and then drying out again, it will soon become cockled and consequently more difficult to use. The pages in a sketchbook will generally survive quite well, even if the paper is of poor quality, because they can be stored closed.

If a drawing is framed, the glass should not be allowed to come in contact with the paper, as changes in humidity will stimulate the growth of bacteria, causing brown spots, or "foxing", to appear. (It is better to use glass in frames rather than perspex,

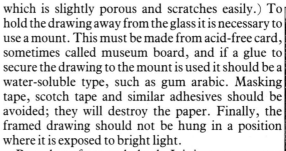

which is slightly porous and scratches easily.) To hold the drawing away from the glass it is necessary to use a mount. This must be made from acid-free card, sometimes called museum board, and if a glue to secure the drawing to the mount is used it should be a water-soluble type, such as gum arabic. Masking tape, scotch tape and similar adhesives should be avoided; they will destroy the paper. Finally, the framed drawing should not be hung in a position where it is exposed to bright light.

Paper has a front and a back. It is important to use the right side, particularly with soft chalk or pastel, because the mechanical texture which distinguishes the back, although not immediately obvious, will show up if lightly drawn over with chalk. This fine mechanical texture, which is impressed by the wire mesh of the mould on which it was made, is not always easy to identify, but if the sheet is held at an angle to the light it will appear in relief. The front may look rougher on many papers, but it lacks this grain.

Artists develop preferences about which papers to use by experiment, and there is a large range of weights and degrees of smoothness from which to choose. A rougher surface tends to be more suitable for chalk and charcoal, as the "nap" or "key" on the surface holds these materials better. Pen and ink is less sympathetic on such a paper, however, as the nib will damage the surface' if the paper is absorbent,

Making paper
1. Shred scraps of waste paper, barely cover them with water and leave to soak overnight. Make a note of the weight of paper used.

2. Put the soaked paper into a liquidizer. Add just enough water to ensure that the machine works smoothly. Liquidize the paper until it forms a pulpy mass.

3. Pour the pulp into a plastic bucket or other suitable container.

4. Measure out a quantity of pulp and pour it into a large vat of water. The proportion of water to fibre should be 99½ : ½ so it is important to have kept note of the weight at each stage of the process.

5. Stir the water in the vat to distribute the pulp. Plunge the paper mould in the vat and immerse it in the solution.

7. Hold the mould at one end of a piece of felt, drop it down flat to release the paper and pull it up quickly from the felt at the other end.

8. Lay another sheet of damp felt over the paper. Repeat the process if more than one sheet of paper is being prepared.

9. Put the felt sheets containing the paper into a press and apply heavy, even pressure to squeeze out the surplus water.

10. Take the flat sheets out of the press. Roll back the top layer to expose the sheet of paper.

11. Hold the paper by the top corners and peel it gently away from the felt. The paper will still be damp but it is quite strong at this stage.

6. Bring the mould out of the vat in a horizontal position so that the water drains away leaving an even layer of pulp in the mould. The process of filling the mould should be done in one smooth, quick action.

12. Lay the paper on a sheet of blotting paper and make sure it is completely flat. Allow to dry naturally. Alternatively, dry the paper in a small photographic print drier. Finally, coat the paper with size.

Above *Terraced Houses* In this subject, the interest lies in the hanging patterns of brickwork and the details of the facades. For a drawing which demands precision and a subtle differentiation of textures, pencil is the ideal medium. A 2B or 3B pencil can make fine lines and is soft enough to give a range of tones. Softer grades can be used to block in black areas. The appeal of this type of work rests on minute observation and the patience to record detail faithfully

Right *Tall Tree, Suffolk* A thoughtful and concentrated pencil study of a solitary tree As a result of careful observation of the directions of the branches, the tree creates its own space around it. A good artist can always be recognized by the ability to avoid any sort of generalization, endowing everything with its own individuality

Several types of eraser are commonly used. A putty rubber is useful for picking out highlights from shaded areas. Modern plastic rubbers and the artgum eraser will remove most lines without smudging. Pencils are available in different grades, from very hard to very soft. Apart from graphite ("lead") pencils, there are also charcoal and carbon pencils and coloured pencils.

the ink will "bleed" and produce a fuzzy line.

The surfaces of good papers are divided into three main categories: Rough, Not and Hot Pressed. Rough is paper with a natural untreated surface, just as it comes off the mould. Not is smoothed a certain amount under pressure, and Hot Pressed (HP) is the smoothest of all. Each of these categories also varies according to the degree of glue size that has been added to the paper. Size controls the absorbency of the paper; the more size the greater its resistance to water. A completely unsized paper is called waterleaf. It is almost as absorbent as blotting paper, has a delicate surface and should be handled gently.

Rather than buying sheets of expensive handmade paper, a good quality cartridge paper is adequate for many types of drawing. There are also other possibilities. Mould-made paper, for example, is made from the same quality materials as handmade, but on a machine and is consequently cheaper.

A sensible choice for outdoor work, is paper bound as a sketchbook. A sketchbook is not as cheap as single sheets, but if it is bound in hard covers and has detachable pages it offers great advantages. It is portable and provides a simple solution to the problem of storage. Although sketchbooks would not be appropriate for delicate work such as pastel, they are good for pen or pencil drawings. Art suppliers should have a choice of sketchbooks containing a variety of different papers. It is sensible to have more than one size, including a pocket sketchbook for the occasions when only rapid little drawings are possible.

Pencil
Pencils offer the most direct means of making marks on paper; most people have been familiar with them in some form or another from their earliest years. The artist is primarily concerned with a pencil's degree of softness. There is normally a choice of 12 grades, from very hard (6H) to very soft (6B). Although fairly hard pencils may be used for fine and delicate work on occasions, they have certain disadvantages. They can only make pale lines of limited variation in strength, and the strongest line will involve exerting a fair amount of pressure, which will indent the surface of the paper. Such a line is impossible to erase completely. The softest pencils, on the other hand, while they are capable of smooth dark lines, have the minor disadvantages of needing frequent sharpening, and also tend to smudge easily. A 2B or 3B pencil is a good balance, but many people prefer something softer. Pencils with thick leads, which are particularly suitable for filling in dark areas, are also available in different grades.

It is not really fruitful to make general statements about how to begin drawing, because often the most lively and also most personal work results from not thinking too hard about the exact nature of the marks you are making. However, it is usually better to begin with tentative lines. These can always be made more emphatic, and it is often interesting to see where an artist has changed his mind as his observations have consolidated. To make too much use of an eraser if lines seem wrong can interrupt the directness of expression which the pencil can achieve so well. It could also be argued that to erase a mistake so that it is no longer visible, is not going to increase one's chances of getting it right next time. A better approach would be to see every mark as part of the whole process of exploration.

Silverpoint, rarely used today, is a method of

Pencil effects Using different grades of pencil on different types of paper gives a wide variety of effects.
1. A soft pencil (4B) is useful for making a graduated tone on fairly smooth paper.
2. A 4B pencil on rough paper gives a rougher result.
3. If the reverse end of a pencil is used to make indentations on the paper, the marks will show up when drawn over.

4. Erasers can be used in a positive way not just to remove errors. They are particularly effective for creating highlights.
5. Wax pencils, such as Chinagraphs, reveal the texture of the paper.
6. A dense black or grey tone can be made by smudging soft pencil dust with the fingers.

Pencil grades
Eight different grades of pencil were shaded across a piece of paper in varying tones to show the differences between grades. The pencils were *(top to bottom)*: 10H, 7H, 3H, 2H, HB, 3B, 6B, and EE.

drawing made with a piece of silver on paper which has been coated with an opaque white pigment. The line produced is ineradicable, and consequently this type of drawing demands greater deliberation.

Some varieties of coloured pencil are also useful to the artist, particularly the Prismalo range, as they are water soluble. They can be used for straightforward coloured drawings, or brushed over with water to obtain washes. The pencils themselves can be moistened to produce a softer line. They are naturally harder than proper watercolour pigments so they are not a rival to that medium, but they can be used for similar effects on a small scale.

Pen and ink

The lines made by a pen have a much more incisive quality than those of any other drawing medium. None of the more recently developed tips made of fibre, for example, however fine, can match the clean sharpness given by the metal nib. It is becoming more and more difficult to find an extensive selection of nibs of the sort which fit into a separate handle, made specifically for artists, but this difficulty is offset to some extent by the increasing number of complete pens now on the market. For those who prefer but cannot obtain the more traditional variety, a fountain pen with an italic nib is quite a good substitute for the dip pen. The thickness of the line can be varied by the angle of the nib, as with dip pens, and these pens do give a more even flow of ink. Even so, fitting a new nib into its handle, dipping it into a pot of ink and carefully calculating the amount of liquid it can hold without blotting does have a certain appeal. It also imposes a discipline and rhythm which is both stimu-

Above *Storm 3* This evocative ink drawing exploits the dramatic theme of stormy weather by using the full contrast of black Chinese ink and the white of the paper. The artist used a brush, together with other improvised drawing materials, such as a rag and a twig, to achieve this atmospheric result.
Right Pen and ink is particularly effective for representing the bleak landscape of winter. In this drawing of a farm building the ink lines are softened with a wash.

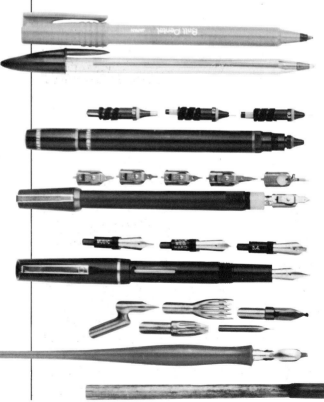

Left Almost any type of pen can be used for drawing, although the traditional dip pens, where the nib fits into a separate handle, will always retain their appeal for the artist.

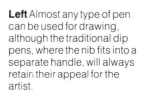

lating and technically satisfying.

Care must be taken when buying ink to check its permanence. Even reputable manufacturers sell inks, especially coloured ones, which can fade surprisingly quickly. They are not usually sold with any grading, and should be considered "fugitive" unless otherwise labelled. This is a common problem with most inks found in felt-tipped pens, which also tend to run out surprisingly quickly, but there are exceptions. Some pens made for designers contain permanent inks and give precise control over the thickness of line.

An extension of pen and ink drawing is to use a brush to spread the ink out into either solid dark masses or paler washes. Inks or watercolours can be used. Sable brushes are generally the best for this purpose; they retain their shape well and have a firm but springy quality which gives good control. They must be washed out very thoroughly after use, as dried ink at the base of the hairs will cause them to splay.

Charcoal and chalk

Both chalk and charcoal are much softer than the softest pencil and are more suitable for work on a larger scale, A black chalk or charcoal can give areas of a rich, velvety nature, but since the medium is so soft it must be held onto the paper with fixative. The tenuous bond between charcoal and paper before it is fixed means that the eraser can be used in a positive way to take out darkened areas to get back to white.

Chalk and charcoal are well suited to the creation of light and dark masses, rather than the more linear compositions for which a pen or pencil is better. As

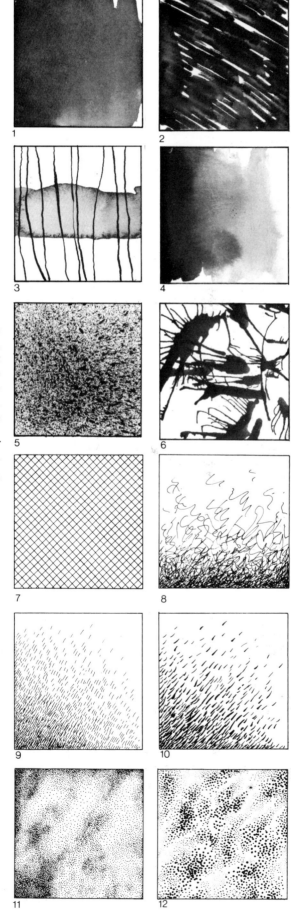

Right *Pen and ink effects*
1. An ink wash and brush can be used for graduated tones.
2. A wet paintbrush drawn through thick ink lines gives a blurred effect.
3. A combination of wash and line can be created by drawing a wet brush over ink lines.
4. A graduated wash can be made by laying a block of tone and feathering it out with a wet brush.
5. Ink can be spattered with a toothbrush. A softer effect will be achieved if the ink is then blotted.
6. Wet ink can be blown across the paper using a straw, to give spidery marks.
Stylo tip effects
7. A criss-cross pattern drawn with a stylo tip is even.
8. Scribbles can be effective.
9. Use a fine nib for these dashes.
10. A thicker nib gives a heavier pattern.
11. Dotting with a fine nib is one way of creating a varied tone.
12. This effect is achieved by dotting with different nibs.

soon as the paper becomes broken up into dark and white shapes it becomes much more important to consider the drawing in relation to the whole area and proportion of the paper, and to see the whiteness of the paper positively rather than merely as a background. This white can be thought of as another tone at the artist's disposal, and its shapes considered as carefully as the shapes made by the charcoal. The effect can also be achieved by using white chalk, but it is more rewarding to try to make the white paper itself function as a colour.

Charcoal can be obtained in sticks of various diameters, from very thin to the much thicker pieces used by scene painters. The most popular charcoal stick is made from willow. One of the characteristics of charcoal is that it is extremely brittle so it must be handled very gently. There have been attempts to make charcoal pencils, bound in wood, but these are on the whole unsatisfactory as the charcoal has to be compressed and consequently loses its particular quality. Chalk or crayon, on the other hand, being a manufactured medium, is pleasing and easy to use in this form. Chalks are available in varying degrees of hardness, so some experiment is advisable. A good type is Conté, which comes in black, brown or red. A strong paper should be used and the surface should not be too smooth or the chalk will skid. Fixative must always be carried, for use as soon as the work is finished. It is particularly important to remember this point when using charcoal for sketchbook drawings on location. Fixative is available in aerosol cans or bottles with folding sprays from art suppliers.

Below The effects of charcoal vary according to the type used and the surface of the paper. Here a range of charcoal sticks was drawn across a variety of surfaces, from rough textured handmade paper to smooth machine made cartridge. Charcoal is available in pencil form or sticks. Sticks come in varying widths and all types of charcoal are available in soft, medium and hard.

Charcoal effects
1. Fine hatched lines build up an area of tone. Work in one direction.

2. Loose crosshatching is useful for indicating texture.

8. To make an erased texture, first draw a thick black line.

9. Work the black line into a pattern using a putty eraser. Do not erase the line completely.

Far left *Mother's Roses* This image uses the full richness of the velvety black that charcoal can give. One of the strengths of the composition is that as the artist has related the forms of the plants to each other, they have also been related from the beginning to the whole area of the paper. The vitality of the surface is due, too, to the use of black and white as positive and negative in turn; in some places black shapes are seen against a white ground and in other places this is reversed. In the process, the forms have shed their more literal meaning but gained in form.

Left *Boxted* The artist has here used charcoal for its softer tones of grey. The drawing is firm but with a minimal use of line – the shapes being given a tonal value to establish their relationship with others. It is impossible to separate the appeal of an image from the means with which it was made. Here the artist's observation of gentle variations of tone in the landscape is ideally suited to the medium employed.

3. Broad areas of tone, revealing the texture of the paper, can be made with the side of the charcoal stick.

4. Working in line over the top of a broad area of tone creates a richer texture.

5. A softer effect can be achieved by smudging charcoal dust with the fingers.

6. A soft putty rubber can be used to erase or work in extra texture.

7. A plastic rubber is useful for creating highlights of fine lines.

10. To make a charcoal wash, first complete the drawing in line and tone.

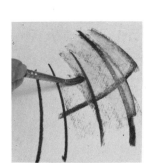

11. Apply a wash with a moistened brush, spreading the tonal areas.

12. Allow the wash to dry before further work.

13. White chalk or pastel is effective to highlight on tinted paper.

14. Fixative is essential to prevent the drawing from smudging. Spray lightly.

Richmond Weir

charcoal on paper 20 x 26 inches (51 x 66 cm)

The attraction of this image for the artist was that the eye, having first been drawn by the white foaming water tumbling down from the weir, is then directed further back in space by the equally bright, but absolutely smooth surface of the river above the weir. Charcoal was chosen because the idea was a specifically tonal one. Charcoal also provides an excellent means of covering large areas with tone very quickly; this is important when working out of doors in uncertain weather.

The weir itself has been simplified as a silhouette, and the sky has been made darker than was literally the case, in both instances to intensify the whiteness of the water. The composition has been organized so that we get some feeling for the space between ourselves and the weir. This intention can often lead to rather large expanses of foreground, but in this case the swirling water provided another contrast with the absolutely flat surface of the river beyond the weir.

Charcoal is a bold medium, best suited to emphatic lines and heavy areas of tone. Because it is powdery and unstable it can be difficult to control at first, but with practice it will be found most rewarding, especially for large drawings or quick sketches showing a scene in terms of light and shade. A thin charcoal stick is first used lightly to sketch out the basic lines of the composition (1, 2) showing simple shapes and the main directionals across the picture plane. The dark tones of bridge and background detail are then loosely blocked in with vigorous hatching. The structure of the composition is developed with heavy linear marks along the horizon line, reinforced with patches of tone laid in with the tip and side of the charcoal stick (3, 4). The shapes are gradually elaborated.

3

1

2

7

4

The advantage of the crumbly, loose character of a charcoal stick is that an eraser can be used freely as a means of developing the drawing, rather than just to eliminate mistakes. To build up the tones the black, powdery material can be spread lightly with a rag or fingers and white areas reclaimed with the eraser (5). This technique is used here to indicate the broad sweep of water in front of the weir. The background is built up with a combination of lines and flourishes representing trees and bushes interwoven with grainy, scribbled marks and dense patches of tone, laid with the long side of the stick. The weir is described in greater detail, contrasting the sharp lines of the man-made structure with the heavy mass of trees behind. As the drawing progresses the shapes are reworked and darkened to emphasize tonal contrasts in the image (6). This also gives a variety of textures in the drawing. Parts become almost black while an uneven, grainy grey fills the sky and is echoed lightly in the water. Drawing materials such as charcoal and pencil are essentially linear and this quality is apparent even in areas of heavy shading, giving a complex network of interacting marks which must become cohesive in the final image (7).

5

6

A 2B pencil is used here which is soft enough for shading in areas of tone but can be used with some precision to establish the linear basis of the composition *(1)* and in developing detail. The main vertical and horizontal lines are put in, linked by curving shapes noted briefly at first. Light hatching establishes some tonal depth *(2)*.

Woods

pencil on paper 20 x 26 inches (51 x 66 cm)

One of the artist's objectives here has been to define the forms of the trees and undergrowth without them becoming too subordinate to the effects of light, which comes from an unseen source. The light, however, is an important part of the image; the path leads out of the wood and we are intended to follow it in our imagination. The artist has had to seek a balance between expressing the theme of darkness within the wood, and at the same time give the trees and plants sufficient solidity to establish their positions in space. Consequently, the lines which delineate some of the tree trunks in the foreground, and the broad leaves on the ground, are given more weight than if they had been seen in an exclusively tonal manner. The flexibility of the marks made by a fairly soft pencil has been exploited to this end, outlines being legible within broad areas of shading.

2

3

1

4

5

In the final stages those parts of the image which define the overall structure should be reinforced and details sharpened to provide focal points in the drawing. A detail of the foreground (6) shows how certain lines are reworked to draw out a particular form from the vigorous mass of marks. A heavy black pencil with a thick point may be used in addition to the 2B to vary the tone and texture of the marks.

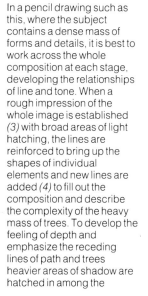

In a pencil drawing such as this, where the subject contains a dense mass of forms and details, it is best to work across the whole composition at each stage, developing the relationships of line and tone. When a rough impression of the whole image is established (3) with broad areas of light hatching, the lines are reinforced to bring up the shapes of individual elements and new lines are added (4) to fill out the composition and describe the complexity of the heavy mass of trees. To develop the feeling of depth and emphasize the receding lines of path and trees heavier areas of shadow are hatched in among the vertical lines (5). Criss-cross marks and short, emphatic lines are put in to show grass and plants around the base of the trees in the foreground. Working across the image strengthening the marks or redefining particular shapes allows control of the overall view so the forms of trees, bushes and plants emerge gradually and the drawing has a continual harmony. Each layer of tone should be carefully placed to clarify the three-dimensional nature of the forms and suggest surface texture and the fall of light.

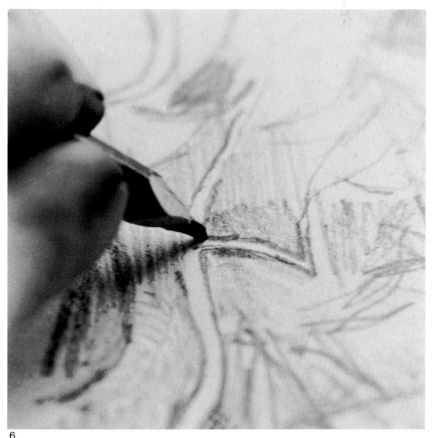

6

The Bridge

pencil on paper 15 x 20 inches (38 x 51 cm)

An architectural subject can present a simple, almost abstract composition, for example in the smooth lines and flat surfaces of modern buildings, or a random, complex arrangement of pattern, tone and colour. This may be as intricate as anything found in nature, although fixed within a basic geometric structure. A wealth of visual stimuli is provided for the artist in the contrast of old and new buildings, smooth stone or glass walls against ageing bricks and ironwork, and the natural earth colours of traditional building materials interrupted by brightly painted doors, street signs or advertising hoardings. A drawing in pencil or charcoal, as here, may deal with the linear emphasis, broad planes and heavy shadows while a painting is obviously more suitable if interest lies mainly in the rich colours seen under summer light or the subtlety of wintry greys and neutral tones. Rules of perspective may be found useful in this type of work, but close observation of the network of shapes and the way the elements interlock is fundamentally more valuable. Much of the pleasure in such a subject lies in unexpected effects, caused by the differences in height and structure among the buildings, heavy cast shadows touched by rays of light striking between roofs or walls, and decorative devices incorporated in the shapes, whether by accident or design as the site has evolved and developed.

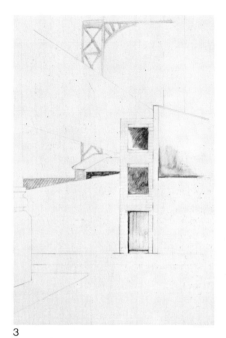

3

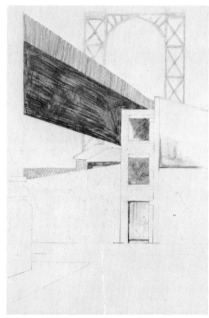

4

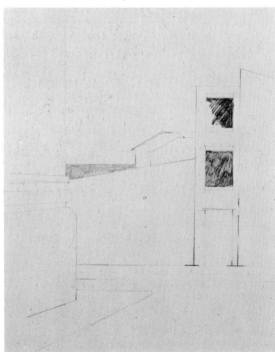

1

An architectural subject should be carefully planned and there is no harm in using a ruler to trace out the basic composition. When firm guidelines have been established (1), the drawing can be continued freehand as too much reliance on a ruler will lead to a rigid, lifeless drawing. A 2B pencil is used here on soft paper with a fairly heavy grain so that broad areas of dense tone can be built up.

2

5

8

7

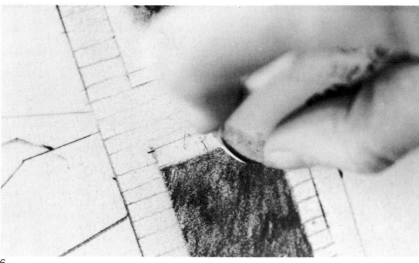

6

The jumble of urban landscape produces interesting combinations of tone and pattern within a basically geometric structure. The basic outline establishes this composition and areas of tone are blocked in directly. Patterns such as brickwork and the iron bridge are lightly drawn in line and shaded, loosely at first and then more strongly to build up a range of greys and blacks, for example in the dark windows of the central building (2). A range of tones is established in this central area within the pencil grid (3) and the darkest tone is then put in to establish a key. This is the heavy black band of the bridge which cuts through the image (4). Greys in the background are added, completing the horizontal and vertical lines of the bridge (5). Details of the buildings below are strengthened, using an eraser where necessary to clean up white shapes (6). As the drawing progresses the tones are unified by further work, showing the pattern of bricks and heavy shadows on the walls to the left of the image (7). Another dark patch of tone showing a doorway on the righthand side is broken up with detail (8) and also serves to balance the dominant shapes in the bridge.

Olive Grove

pen and ink on paper   8 x 12 inches (20 x 30 cm)

The particular character of some landscapes will often prompt the use of a particular medium. The twisted and spiky quality of the olive trees has led the artist to exploit the type of spiky marks possible with pen and ink. He has used the trunks of the trees and their shadows on the ground to create a sort of broken grid as a way of defining the spatial extent of the grove.   The sparse shadows almost directly under the trees have been used to express the position of the sun, and the rather leisurely figure of the shepherd to express the heat.

Pen and ink invites an economical statement, but the silhouetted leaves and branches at the top were made by letting generous drops of ink fall onto the paper. These were then dispersed with rapid movements of the pen.

3

It is difficult to correct an ink drawing successfully so the medium requires a confident and disciplined approach. The subject must necessarily be one which can be broken down in terms of line, pattern and texture but although the marks made with pen and ink are characteristically linear, a great deal of variation can be achieved between thick and thin, fluid or crisp lines. A useful way to start is to draw in a loose outline of a central object, for example the spreading tree in this image (1) and put in a few lines to show the layout of the drawing as a whole. Building on this the forms can be elaborated to identify the rhythmic structure of the composition (2). Although the approach is direct nothing should be put in at this stage which eliminates areas of further development in the image. The detail (3) shows how the composition progresses from left to right in a sketchy, open manner

1

2

5

4
When the basic design of the drawing is simply mapped out each area can be more fully treated with pattern and texture, using hatched lines and brisk, fluid marks. This builds up the tonal density in the work, equivalent to shaded areas in a pencil drawing, which defines three-dimensional form, light and shade and the impression of space and distance (4). Small patches of cast shadow beneath the trees emphasize the horizontal plane as it recedes from the viewer. This throws into relief the vertical and angled forms of the trees. In the final stage the lines are strengthened and more detail is added to suggest the pattern of branches and foliage (5). The strokes of the pen can be made quite boldly (6).

6

Pastel

Pastel is a medium which hovers finely between painting and drawing. It offers the most direct way of getting pure coloured pigment onto a surface. The pigment is bound tightly with gum arabic, or occasionally tragacanth, and then moulded into sticks, but so lightly that it crumbles onto the surface with the minimum of pressure. It is this delicacy which gives pastel both its beauty and its numerous technical problems. The softness of the pastel requires great care from the moment it is first picked up until after the work has been framed.

Colour

One of the aims of the pastellist is to use the pigment in its purest and most direct form, and this must influence his approach to colour. Although it is quite possible to mix colours, the desired freshness and directness can suffer; in any case, there is less need to mix as pastels are light and compact, and more can be carried than tubes of oil paint. Where the painter will mix his own colours from a relatively small number of tubes, the pastellist can select appropriate colours from an enormous range to suit the demands of a particular work. It may well be that only a dozen pigments are employed for one picture, no more than the painter has on his palette, but another subject may suggest an entirely different set of pastels. Where the painter would make different mixtures

from the same basic palette the pastellist is better advised to carry a wider variety of colours.

There are hundreds of colours available in pastel, often only barely discernible from one another, and a choice may well seem impossible when seeing the full range on display. (Ten different whites are available.) However difficult the choice, it is probably not worth buying a box of pastels as these selections tend to contain too many bright strong colours at the expense of intermediate ones. Whether some bright colours are used or not, it is the indeterminate greys, soft greens and ochres which are eventually the most useful. For landscape and nature subjects, it should almost be a policy to buy those very colours which are most difficult to describe, those pearly blue-greys, warm silvery pinks and pepper and salt colours, which we find so beguiling in nature. It is best to acquire an assortment of such colours gradually and have a more sparing collection of the bright primaries.

As with any other medium which involves the use of colour, it is important to aim for a good balance of warm and cool colours, for this dimension of colour is the one which can best express the play of light on the landscape. A tonal variety is also necessary, but pastel is a medium where the value of a colour change can be most telling. Because of the powdery, granular nature of the pigment, it cannot attain quite the same

Left There is a wide range of pastels on the market; Sennelier and Rembrandt are two well-known brands. Although many manufacturers produce box sets, it is not always advisable to buy pastels this way. It is often better to choose pastels separately, even from different manufacturers if necessary, and aim to build up an extensive collection of shades in the colours that most appeal to you. Because pastels are not easy to mix and they are so light and compact, it is easy enough to carry a wide range of colours.
Pastels are also available in pencil form, known as carbon pencils. These are not as popular as the stick variety. Although they are easy to handle and not so messy to use, they are quite soft and break easily.

Left Keeping families of colours in separate boxes is a good way of ensuring that pastels remain clean. Because pastels are so soft, they pick up dirt easily.

tonal range as an oil painting.

There are several makes of pastel which can be highly recommended; Sennelier and Rembrandt are both good choices. Pastels are very fragile, and it is worth developing a storage system. Because a painter has relatively few tubes of paint to organize, these can be thrown into a box without suffering any damage, but the pastellist works with a far greater number of delicate colours, which also must be kept clean. A good system is to collect a large quantity of small cardboard boxes, preferably with linings of corrugated paper to hold the pastels in place. A foam rubber padding will prevent the pastels from jolting and getting broken when they are carried around, and the boxes should be secured with a rubber band.

There is also the problem of keeping the pastels clean, as being so soft they can both rub off on one another and also pick up dirt from elsewhere. Dusting them with flour is often recommended, but there is a tendency for the flour to cling to the pigment too much. A better suggestion is to sprinkle a little rice, well-known for its absorbency, into each box.

Whether such refinements are employed or not, it is a good idea to divide the pastels into groups of colour, each with its own box. Each box should contain a family of colours; cool whites, warm whites, blue-greys, green-greys, pink-greys, violets, reds, blues, yellows, sand colours, browns and so on.

Some notion of the range of colours available can be gained from this display. Pastels are also made in three qualities: soft, medium and hard. Manufacturers usually label pastels with the name of the colour and a number to indicate the relative lightness or darkness of tone. There is no standard system, but a scale of 0 to 8 is often used, with 0 being the lightest shade.

Left *Sketchbook study*, J.M.W. Turner. Turner was an artist who constantly switched from one medium to another. He loved experiment and paid no great attention to the conventions of his time in matter of either technique or subject. Here we can see the boldness with which he used pastel; he sometimes turned to this medium in the evenings when the light became too subdued for him to work with watercolour. He frequently favoured working on dark paper. As light was one of his major preoccupations he liked it to be present in his work as the result of a positive statement with brush or chalk.

Pastel techniques
1. Press firmly using the side of the pastel to obtain broad, diagonal strokes.

2. Rubbing lines with the fingertips gives a hazy look to pastel hatching.

3. To achieve crisp fine lines, use the side of the pastel and apply light pressure.

4. Another set of fine lines, worked in the opposite direction, gives cross-hatching.

5. Broad areas can be worked by using the blunt end of the pastel. Work in one direction only, applying firm, even pressure.

6. To lay a broad, grainy area, peel away the protective paper and use the long side of the pastel.

7. A putty eraser, kneaded to a point, can be used to lift the pastel and create highlights.

8. A stippled effect can be obtained by using the blunt end of the pastel to make brisk strokes across the paper.

Paper

An important part of these decisions about colour is the choice of paper. It is rare to use a white; there is a particular satisfaction to be derived from using a colour which is itself part of the whole colour scheme. Areas of the paper can be left untouched, thus contributing to the overall harmony. It is possible to buy paper in quite a good range of colours, preferably warm greys, cool greys and green-greys; again, the soft colours which are hard to describe. The paper must be of good quality, mould-made if not hand-made. It should be sized and fairly thick. Too soft a surface will get damaged and not permit alterations. It is particularly important to establish which is the front side of the paper, as the mechanical texture of the back will soon appear when the pastels are applied. Ingres and Canson are two makes of paper which are very suitable; there is also a paper sold specifically for pastel, aptly called Pummice. This has a hard granular surface, which is too hard for some tastes. An ordinary Not or Rough surface is normally satisfactory; Hot Pressed can be a little too smooth. It is important for the paper to have enough "tooth" to rasp off the pastel.

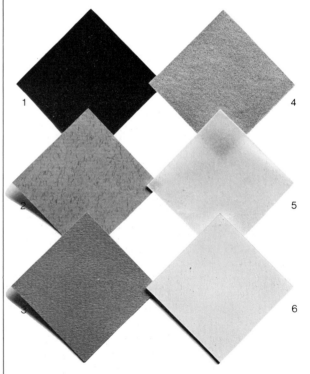

Above A number of different papers are suitable for pastel work. Paper must have enough "tooth" to rasp off the pastel as it is drawn across the surface. Tinted paper is particularly effective, as some areas can be left to provide an additional colour. Ingres papers are reliable coloured papers. Fabriano (1), Swedish Tumba (2), and Canson (3) are specially textured Ingres papers, available in a range of colours. Glass paper (4) is a soft, fine paper with a sandpaper surface. Vellum (5, 6) is good for a delicate, detailed approach.

Erasers

Due to the difficulties of covering one colour with another, it is necessary to develop ways of removing pastel from the paper's surface. A painter using oil paint will have his brush in one hand and a rag in the other, so that the construction of the painting is a constant process of addition and subtraction. The same applies to pastel, but a rag alone is not always adequate. A clean dry rag can be used to flick pastel off the paper but it is helpful to have a few other means of erasing. A good quality rubber is essential, and, for finer adjustments, an eraser in stick form. Also useful is a piece of plastic sponge, and because the pigment is dry and is not actually absorbed by the paper it can be brushed off with a paintbrush. This should have fairly stiff bristles such as hog hair, which have been worn down.

Techniques

At all stages, the fragility of the medium must be remembered. When the work is finished, it is desirable to put it in a card mount of some sort so that the surface will be protected. The prospect of mounting the finished work may affect the earlier planning of the composition: if the edges of the paper are going to be lost anyway, the proportions of the work need not correspond exactly with the proportions of the paper. Allowing for a border means that the paper may be held with clips onto a drawing board and the edge can be used for trying out colours. The border may be an equal distance in from the edge of the paper all around, but if the proportions of the picture are to be materially different from that of the paper this should be established at an early stage. If necessary, draw the border lightly onto the paper as the composition is worked out. With almost any medium, there can be a temptation to start a picture as a vignette – that is, an image with undefined borders – but this should be resisted. Working on coloured paper, the pastellist may find this tendency more pronounced; the feelings of space and light have to be created by the colour, where on a white surface they may be implicit.

With pastel, a tentative drawing may be made on the paper with a neutral colour Conté crayon, but the decisions about which colours to use simply cannot be deferred. If a colour is wrong it is best to remove it altogether, which may well be advisable with paint

Below *Wooded Landscape*, Thomas Gainsborough. Gainsborough's techniques were considered somewhat unorthodox by his contemporaries but his work had a freshness which gained him many admirers. This freshness he managed to bring even to the landscapes he drew or painted in the studio. He had a major place as a portrait painter but his real love was landscape, which he composed and invented in a variety of media. He anticipated Constable in his portrayal of the everyday rural scene, but possibly because he spent less time working on the spot than Constable was to do, his later landscapes tended towards the picturesque.

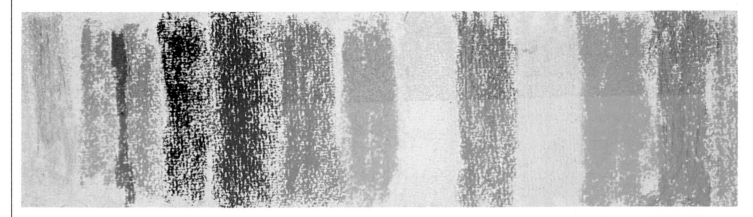

Above The use of fixative alters the appearance of pastel drawings, making the colours appear darker. However, not all colours are darkened to the same degree and relationships between colours can therefore be affected. Some fixing is necessary, however or a great deal of pigment will be lost from the surface.

Right *Trees*. Lawrence Toynbee. Oil pastels are not yet manufactured in such a wide range of colours as the more traditional pastels bound with gum. This need not be a disadvantage as the building of form is always more important than copying the colours we see. Lawrence Toynbee is perhaps best known for his sporting pictures, but he has also made many fine landscapes in paint and pastel.

too, but the pastellist has much less latitude. A colour can never be totally obliterated by another.

Where a painter starts by putting little dabs of the main colours to be used on the canvas, the pastellist tries out the colours with each other on the edge of the paper. He must make a selection from the many different colours at his disposal to meet the demands of each separate subject, and it is very unlikely that he will use anything like as many as his full collection. At this stage, it is useful to have a few empty boxes at hand so that the pastels tried out and chosen are easily available.

Once a pastel has been chosen and is identifiable from the mark on the edge of the paper, it can then be unwrapped and used on its side if need be. It is not practicable to sharpen pastels. If a finer line is needed, the pastel can be broken in two to give a sharp corner to work with.

It is possible to mix colours to some extent by working one colour into another which has already been applied to the paper. If this is done too much, however, there is a danger of the colours losing their brilliance. One of the main reasons for working in pastel is that it is one of the most direct ways of applying pigment, so it is worth considering other methods which will reduce the need to rub colours together. For an area which one feels has elements of several different colours, pastel is well suited to a divisionist approach, that is, breaking up the area into its different component colours in minute juxtaposition, without rubbing them all together. The subsequent colour will be mixed in the eye rather than on the paper. This technique need not be quite so methodical as Seurat's Pointillisme, where each dot of colour was carefully calculated in size, and the whole was intended to be viewed from a specific distance. Used in a freer fashion, it can often bring an area to life and give it more sparkle than an area of flat colour, especially if the colour of the paper is also contributing.

Changing media can give artists new insights, and the switch from paint to pastel, and the other way round, could be instructive in the area of colour mixing. With pastel, there is a wide range of colour to be picked up and applied. With paint, the colour has to be made on the palette. Both ways of working are difficult, but attempting the two different approaches can teach a great deal about colour in general.

Some controversy exists among pastel artists over the use of fixative, a thin varnish suspended in a fast evaporating spirit which holds the pastel to the paper. It is generally acknowledged that some fixing is necessary, although the purist would keep this to an absolute minimum, with the good reason that it has a dulling effect on the surface. Before the pastel is fixed, the tiny particles of pigment lie at different angles, reflecting light from every direction. When they are sprayed with the varnish, these particles seem to subside and lie more evenly, no longer displaying that original sparkle. The other reason for resisting the use of fixative is that it darkens the colour. This would be slightly more acceptable if all colours were darkened to the same degree, but some pigments change just a little, others much more dramatically. This can radically alter relationships between colours which have been carefully established. However, without fixative, even a light jolt can cause a fair quantity of pigment to fall off the surface. Manet once made a pastel drawing on canvas, which, being a more flexible support than mounted paper, soon shed almost the entire work.

One compromise solution is to fix the work lightly in stages as it progresses. This has a double advantage. It enables the artist to assess the degree to which his colours will darken before the work is finished so he can make the necessary adjustments as he goes along, and also it permits a more vigorous restating of lines or masses without reducing the colours to an indeterminate mess. Some freshness will be sacrificed by this method, but a richness can be gained.

Those who use pastel more as a drawing medium, especially if they work vigorously and are constantly making alterations without erasing what is already on the paper, are forced to make more use of fixative. Edgar Degas experimented continually with such technical problems. Not only did he test the advantages and disadvantages of fixing the pastel at various stages, he also tried soaking his paper in turpentine

Oil pastels are quite different from pure "true" pastels. They are stronger and less brittle, and because they are harder, can be sharpened to a point with a knife. Oil pastels are usually available in a set – a typical medium-sized selection is shown here. They are useful for sketches, for the preparatory work in oil painting, and can also be combined with watercolour washes to give an interesting effect.

before working on it. His work is very well preserved.

It is worth experimenting both with different methods of fixing pastels and with different fixative preparations. Fixative can be applied with a spray, or atomizer, or from an aerosol can. The paper must be laid down on a flat surface, and it is important not to get the point of the vaporizer too close.

Fixative is basically a form of shellac dissolved in alcohol or methylated spirits. White shellac can be put in a small muslin bag which is suspended in pure grain alcohol. The shellac will dissolve and sink to the bottom of the container, leaving the shellac in the bag in contact with fresh alcohol. It will take a matter of days for all the shellac to dissolve, then the solution is filtered to remove impurities and sealed in a bottle. The proportion of shellac to alcohol is one part shellac to ten parts alcohol. To increase the permanence of the fixative, copal resin can be added to the above mixture in the following proportions: ⅜ oz (5g) white shellac, ⅜ oz (5g) pulverized copal resin and 1 pint (.6 l) alcohol. A cheaper version is to mix white shellac varnish in equal parts with methylated spirits.

An alternative to shellacs and resins is the casein from milk; some people simply use milk. An old method of ensuring the permanence of documents written in pencil was to dip the paper in skimmed milk, but a pastel could not be treated in this way. A recommended recipe based on casein is: ¾ oz (10g) casein, ³⁄₂₀ oz (2g) borax, ¾ pint (.4l) water, and ¼ pint (.12l) pure grain alcohol.

First, a little of the water is added to the casein and borax. After a few hours this mixture will turn to syrup, which is then diluted with the remaining water. The alcohol is then added and the solution is left to stand and clarify. It is then decanted and bottled.

It is advisable to mount a pastel as soon as it is finished and fixed. The mount must be made of acid-free card, or museum board, and should be as thick as possible. The pastel should be fixed onto a solid piece of backing card, with the window mount hinged to form the front. The firm backing will protect the back of the work and keep the paper as flat and rigid as possible. No part of the front of the paper need be glued. The glue used to secure the paper to the backing card should be water-soluble, such as gum arabic. Sellotape and masking tape should be avoided at all costs, but other types of tape made with a harmless adhesive are available. Experiment with different sizes and colours of mounting board. Usually, a colour which enhances one of the pastel colours is most suitable, although white can set off a tinted paper.

Left *Sky/Sea 10, Corton.*
This work, which expresses
the fusion of the sea and sky,
is an excellent example of an
artist seizing on the value of
an unexpected opportunity.
Chalk, charcoal, watercolour
and Chinese ink have been
used, and even raindrops
were incorporated when they
began to fall when the work
was in progress.

Left Oil pastel is very
effective combined with
watercolour washes. First,
rub oil pastel over
watercolour paper to give a
grainy pattern (1). Lay a
watercolour wash over the
pastel (2). The oil will repel
the watercolour, which
settles into the grain of the
paper.

Poppies in Haute Provence

pastel on paper 6 x 4 inches (15 x 10 cm)

Pastels offer the qualities of both drawing and painting media – they can be used for linear results or directly applied in shapes of colour. This work shows a very painterly approach; all the drawing has been done with delicate touches of pigment. The treatment of the chosen motif is quiet, almost intimate, and its qualities are dependent on the subtle juxtaposition of colours. There has been no attempt to give the landscape more drama than the colour itself conveys. The composition is based on an intuitive feeling for the placing of one colour next to another, rather than any formal geometric or linear scheme.

This composition is a good example of an artist having decided exactly what it is in the scene which has prompted a response, then keeping that idea as the predominant guiding factor throughout the work. There is no feeling that she has introduced any element which is not intrinsic to the enjoyment of the poppies' colour. The blue-greens of the hills behind complement the warm reds of the flowers, as the mauvish elements of the background complement the warm greens of the grass in the foreground. The flicker of light enlivens the whole landscape.

1

A pastel drawing may be made on tinted paper so that traces of the paper which show through the finished work provide a middle tone. In the initial stages establish the composition by showing the broad bands of sky, horizon, middle ground and foreground. Make loose, sketchy marks in colours appropriate to elements in gradually made more descriptive (1). Srokes of yellow and sage green are used to create the structure in the foliage and are linked with the colours of the sky. Small marks of pink and red indicate the flowers and the middle ground is loosely blocked in.

the landscape. At first, identify the darkest tones and most vivid colours. Here the rhythms in the landscape are put in with olive green, black and touches of red which show the poppies. The sky is blocked in with grainy masses of cobalt and cerulean blue and a warm, light mauve. As the drawing progresses the colours are

Colours

cobalt blue	light olive green	red
cerulean blue	dark olive green	deep rose pink
light pink	yellow	salmon pink
light mauve	raw sienna	
blue-gray	brown	

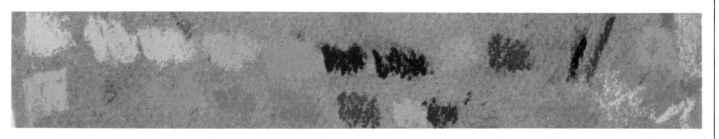

2

The drawing must be allowed to build up slowly or the powdery colours will mix and become unmanageable. Avoid resting the hand on the paper or the drawing will be smudged. Alterations can be made by lifting the colour with a stiff, dry brush and a small eraser. As the image is filled out with colours worked one over another, check the overall balance of tones. Be wary of heavy accents of light and dark which may appear exaggerated. Place bright colours and highlights carefully. For example, the red of the poppies dominates the foreground but crisp touches of pure colour are offset against hazy patches of pink and red emerging through the green foliage. Establish a sense of distance by reducing the distinctions between one element and another at the horizon line. This has been achieved here (2) by overlaying dark colours with a light pink.

Evening Light, Grand Canal

pastel on paper 8½ x 5½ inches (21 x 14 cm)

The buildings and canals of Venice have held the attention of artists since the Renaissance, and the quality of light that pervades this water-bound city must be one of its most consistent attractions. Here the artist concentrated on a cool mood; the buildings have lost the warm colours of midday and acquired a range of silvery qualities.

The principal features of the composition were established with some firm drawing and subsequently built upon with gentle changes of tone. The poles with red stripes in the foreground give a scale both in terms of space and of colour to which the other buildings relate. They form a starting point from which the eye is taken by means of alternating light and dark, and warm and cool colours, towards the domes of the church seen above the rooftops. It is a picture which expresses enjoyment of an unfamiliar view of these domes, so often featured in paintings of Venice, and gives a sense of having turned a corner to discover the unexpected.

Right A composition which includes complex architectural detail must be carefully planned and the initial drawing must be quite elaborate, even though some of the detail may be lost when the work is completed in colour. It is not always possible to work on a full drawing with the subject immediately in view and in this case drawings and notes made in a sketchbook will prove invaluable. A hardback sketchbook with good quality paper provides a firm, smooth surface for pencil drawings made on the spot. These should include as much detail as possible and written notes can be added to record effects of colour and light. Take down all the information about line, colour and tone so you can select particular aspects later for further years.

1

2

Details of the drawing shown in full on the following pages emphasize the importance of a well-observed linear structure as the basis of the composition. The colours are built up with network of small marks following the basic outlines of form and decoration *(1)*. A contrast between warm pink and brown tones and cool blues in varying shades is employed to capture the effect of evening light on the buildings. The intense, light tone of the sky is put in at an early stage, providing a key to highlights and shadows in the rest of the image. Note how the pastel is held at an angle to the paper with the hand hovering just above the surface *(2)*, so the marks can be placed precisely without disturbing previous work. The overall tone of the blue-grey paper provides an underlying harmony to the drawing.

To draw a linear composition finely, it may be convenient to use a chalk or pastel pencil, the type with a wooden casing, which can be sharpened to a point. Make sure it is not greasy or it will be impossible to work freely over the outlines. The image here is drawn in brown on blue-grey paper (1). Cool tones are established first, using light ultramarine and cerulean blue. The lightest part of the sky, directly behind the buildings, is emphasized with pure white to give a cold, clear tone. These colours are extended through the image (2) and offset with warm pink and two shades of brown. The broad masses of buildings and water are built up in simple form, using heavy patches of colour against brief strokes loosely woven into the outlines. As soon as the architectural features are placed the balance of tone and colour can be fully developed.

1

2

Colours

ultramarine	light cerulean blue	light red
light ultramarine	light gray	burnt umber
white	light pink	light burnt sienna

Left An important aspect of this image is the effect of light over the local colours of the buildings, giving a luminous pearly tone to the warm colours. A limited range of colour is used and the tones are linked throughout the different areas of the composition. Pink is used liberally to suggest the delicate colour of stone in the architecture. This is modified with a warm beige in the lefthand side of the drawing. Some distinction is maintained between the blue of sky and canal and the darker tone used to shadow details in the buildings. The foreground is stressed with the heavy shadow to the left and strong detail in bright red, laid in with small, decorative flourishes, showing the boats and landing posts. The directions of the pastel marks help to create a particular form and define the space and structure in the subject generally. The separate tones are gradually merged to harmonize the colours and suggest that the view is given a shimmering, vibrant effect by the evening light.

Puymeras; Overgrown Vines

pastel on paper 7 x 4¾ inches (18 x 12 cm)

Although this pastel contains no strong tonal contrasts, it is nonetheless primarily concerned with light. The shapes of the buildings in the hilltop town are seen over the tangle of vines in the foreground, and the forms of each part of the composition enhance each other by their differences. This does not cut the work in half, as it might have done, because of the bright light which has been observed very consistently as it strikes houses and vegetation alike. It is a high-key light, which conveys heat and unifies the whole. The picture is also unified by touches of the warm pink of the buildings appearing in between the foreground vines.

The artist demonstrates well, in this and her other works, the importance of finding the warm and cool elements in all the colours she uses. The little strokes of warm and cool colour, extended over the whole surface, even in the bright sky, serve to create a mesh whch captures the light.

The picture also shows how an artist's interests operate on different levels at the same time. This picture is of vines and buildings, but equally important is the strong sunlight, which strikes all objects with complete impartiality.

The first stage of this drawing consists of a fairly detailed analysis of the linear structure of the composition (1). The cluster of buildings on the horizon are carefully drawn to give a sound basis for the solid forms. The tangled vines and undergrowth in the foreground are suggested with delicately traced lines and heavier accents which mark the directions and interplay of branches and foliage The paper is again grey, with a blue-green tinge suitable to the main areas of colour which will be added. A few notes at the bottom of the page draw attention to particular aspects of colour and tone to be developed in the drawing. The basic sketch is completed in a neutral tone before local colour is added (2)

1

2

80

3

4

Over the initial drawing the local colour is added and light tones are brought out in the sky, buildings and pathway. White, mauve and a light flesh tone are used for this, with a vivid light blue for the sky (3). The foreground area is loosely blocked in with pale green and then developed with light strokes of blue, mauve and yellow ochre. At this stage the work is kept simple, showing only brief touches of shadow and highlight. The masses of colour are then built up and elaborated (4) to break down broad areas into a more detailed network of shape and colour. The pastel strokes correspond to the interwoven foliage in the foreground. When an overall impression of form and colour emerges the buildings are blocked in more solidly with light tone (5) to emphasize the contrast between the stone surfaces reflecting light and the more complex organic forms below.

5

Watercolour, Gouache and Tempera

Above For making watercolours out of doors, a travelling palette is useful. Separate wells for mixing are essential, so that colours do not flow together. Traditional watercolour palettes are white, usually made of ceramic or enamelled metal. A white palette will enable you to judge the strength of a wash before applying it to the paper.

The term "watercolour" is used in two senses, one of which is more specific than the other. In its broader sense, it simply refers to colours which have been ground up with a water-soluble medium. More specifically, it has come to refer to a way of using such colours so as to exploit their transparent nature. This method, developed primarily by English artists in the eighteenth century, uses the white of the paper on which the painting is done to give colours luminosity. White as a pigment is not used at all. Colours are lightened by further diluting them with water so that they become increasingly transparent, which allows more light to reflect off the white of the paper underneath. This dilution is commonly called a "wash". Where this transparency is not considered desirable, a white pigment can be added, generally Chinese white, which makes the colours more opaque; this is called "gouache".

Watercolour has been used both with and without the addition of white for many hundreds of years. The decoration of medieval manuscripts was done with both transparent and opaque watercolour, the latter preferred for greater richness in conjunction with gold leaf. Only the purist English school of watercolourists made a hard and fast distinction between the use of added white or "body colour", and the transparent form which they preferred, and even amongst this school there was much unorthodox experiment. Turner, for example, frequently used body colour and scratched into the paint with a knife —uses of the medium which the purist would find unacceptable.

Water

Water is a vital element in the process which is often taken for granted. Very hard water often has the effect of precipitating the particles of pigment in the paint, so if the local tap water is hard it is better to collect some rainwater, or, best of all, use distilled water. It is a good idea to have two jars of water, one for mixing with the colour and the other for cleaning brushes.

Gum

The medium with which the pigments are manufactured is gum arabic. This is a misnomer today, as all the acacia trees in the Middle East from which the gum was taken have now died, the water springs which fed them having dried up. Most of the gum now comes from Senegal and South America.

Left *Venice from the Giudecca*, J.M.W. Turner. In contrast to the vigorous style of many of Turner's works, this watercolour has been executed with great delicacy and economy. He has used a limited palette and made very transparent wet washes in a carefully considered and deliberate manner. Fine accents of opaque colour have been added to establish form.

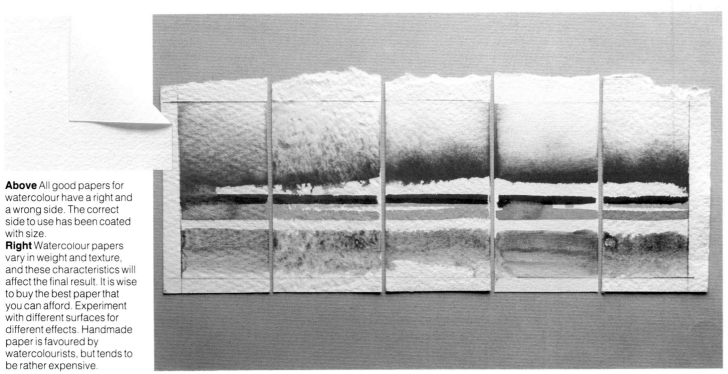

Above All good papers for watercolour have a right and a wrong side. The correct side to use has been coated with size.

Right Watercolour papers vary in weight and texture, and these characteristics will affect the final result. It is wise to buy the best paper that you can afford. Experiment with different surfaces for different effects. Handmade paper is favoured by watercolourists, but tends to be rather expensive.

Because of the different climates of West Africa and Arabia, where the acacia trees were subjected to high temperatures in a dry atmosphere, their water supply being subterranean, there have been some difficulties of manufacture, and the Senegalese gum has to be given an artificial heat treatment.

Water is often the only medium necessary when painting, but sometimes an artist may wish to give the paint more body without changing its colour; this can be achieved by dissolving a little extra gum arabic into the water. This will also increase the adherence of the pigment to the paper.

Different pigments are manufactured with different amounts of gum arabic, and behave differently when they are being applied. It is useful to have some gum to hand, so it can be added when needed. Only the experienced watercolourist will notice the minute differences between colours mixed with smaller or larger amounts of gum, or gum of different qualities, but recognition of them can stimulate experiment. Small quantities of sugar or glycerine can be added to give the paint more body and to delay the drying time. A variety of gums, which all behave slightly differently, can be used.

Gum tragacanth This must be ground to a very fine powder and then dissolved in a tiny amount of pure grain alcohol, or possibly vodka if the alcohol is difficult to obtain. This is best kept in a bottle or jar with a top, so that it can be shaken at intervals.

Rice starch Add 1¾ oz (50 g) of powdered starch to just enough cold water to make a paste. Add the water a little at a time, stirring it to the consistency of cream, and then add this mixture to about half a pint (300 cc) of boiling, preferably distilled, water.

Sarcocolla This is a gum resin which has been used for at least 2,000 years. It is much harder than gum arabic and becomes virtually insoluble when dry. Alcohol is the best solvent, but then it cannot be varnished with an alcohol-based varnish. Unlike other watercolour media, it can be used on top of oil paint and can give brilliant glazes.

Laevulose An extract from honey, laevulose is made by exposing stiff pale honey to the air until it hardens and becomes crystallized. It is then dissoved in alcohol, shaken vigorously and allowed to stand for several hours, shaken again at intervals, and finally filtered.

Glycerine This is a colourless extract from fats, and is easily obtainable.

Brushes

The best brushes for watercolour are made of sable or camel hair, but a large flat hog-hair is also useful for washes. Generally a brush is chosen because it can hold water, yet has enough spring in its hairs to retain its shape, and is capable of forming a fine point. The tendency over the years has been for artists to use smaller brushes, but this may be a way of avoiding the

difficult skills which have given watercolour its appeal, namely the control of a brush charged with a lot of water to give direct and luminous washes. It is worth trying to handle as large a brush as possible, a size 14 or even larger, provided it has a good point. Smaller ones to accompany this could be sizes 8 and 4, which should be adequate to begin with, even if smaller or intermediate sizes are eventually needed.

Other useful equipment includes a small sponge, linen or cotton rags, and blotting paper.

Paper

The quality of paper used by watercolourists is bound to have an important and direct influence on the nature of the work. A heavy, sized, handmade paper is best for watercolour because it holds water well, but a beginner may choose to practice on a good quality cartridge, which is cheaper. However, too poor a paper will give discouraging results. A paper's characteristics, its roughness, absorbency and so on, are very important; every artist becomes increasingly aware of what sort of paper is going to suit his own needs. David Cox (1783-1859), in 1836, found his own ideal in a rough, tinted paper which absorbed his

Left *The White House, Chelsea* (1800), Thomas Girtin. Girtin's work, and particularly this one, was greatly admired by Turner. Girtin was a pioneer of watercolour and extended the medium to new depths and subtleties. This example, painted with a limited range of pigments on buff paper, displays his fine sense of composition and sure eye for tone and colour. It also shows a great sensitivity to the mood and atmosphere of a particular time of day.

washes well. It was actually made as a cheap wrapping paper but, subsequent to his own use of it, was sold specifically for artists. Unfortunately wrapping papers are no longer made from cotton pulp, and there is no good cheap paper available yet. It is wise to accept from the beginning that the quality of paper is just as important as the quality of paint and brushes, and that to economize on any of these things is going to limit the chances of doing good work.

The final choice which each artist makes about paper will depend on the sort of imagery which interests him. It will have to be thick and strong if he is going to scratch and scrub it as Turner did, and have a smooth surface if very fine detail is required. Only experiment will provide the answer. It is best to avoid paper sold in blocks or pads because, for a medium where water can be used in great quantities, the glue which holds the sheets together round the edge is seldom strong enough to keep the paper flat.

To ensure a flat surface, paper can be stretched on a drawing board. When the correct side of the paper has been established, it is dampened evenly all over with a sponge. It need not be flooded with water; the paper should absorb the water without leaving any excess lying in pools on the surface. The paper is then stuck down onto the board all the way round the edge with gumstrip, and allowed to dry naturally, not in the sun or with artificial heat. The surface must of course be kept clean and free of grease.

When a watercolour has been completed and is to be framed behind glass, it is important to ensure that the picture's surface is not in contact with the glass because of the problems of condensation.

Colours

Watercolour paint can be bought either as small, hard cakes or in tubes. The tubes are marginally easier to use especially if working on a large scale, but, although it can be kept moist by the addition of sugar, honey or glycerine, the paint dries quickly on the palette, and using it becomes similar to using the cakes. Many boxes of paint have lids in the form of a palette, which are usually white enamel; alternatively, a few small white saucers can be used. It is important that they are white so that the exact strength of a wash can be assessed before it is put on the paper. It is also helpful to have a few spare scraps of paper for testing colours.

Paints are graded "permanent", "normally permanent" or "durable", "moderately permanent" and "fugitive". An artist may have to settle for less than permanent if he needs a particular colour, but it is best only to buy permanent colours. Although there are a good 60 different colours easily available, it is advisable to start with less than ten. No two artists use exactly the same palette all the time, so there are many variations on the basic palette.

Here are suggestions for a palette containing only completely permanent colours: lemon yellow, yellow ochre, light red, Indian red, raw umber, terre verte, viridian and cobalt blue. Note that neither white nor black are included. It is better, whilst developing a feeling for the medium, to use the paper as the white; this is a time-honoured tradition. A pure black suggests a total absence of light, which is a rare phenomenon, and a near-black can easily be made from a mixture of the blue and raw umber. At some stage a stronger yellow may be needed and this could be cadmium. A brighter red could be alizarin crimson or cadmium again, and other useful additions are raw and burnt sienna, French ultramarine and Hooker's green. It is surprising what a range can be achieved with a few basic pigments, and it is both instructive and enjoyable to mix these colours with each of the others in turn, with varying quantities of water, in order to find different ways of making intermediate shades. Some simple colour mixing exercises can be especially valuable for the discovery of greys, which can be produced from unlikely combinations.

Techniques

One of the first techniques to learn is how to lay a wash, that is, an even, transparent tone which will be illuminated by the paper underneath. It is worth trying this both with the paper dry and with it lightly dampened with a sponge. The quality and texture of the paper will affect the result, an even wash being

Left By far the most popular form of watercolour paint comes in tubes in a semi-liquid state. Dry cakes and semi-moist pans are no longer used a great deal but are still available. Fully liquid watercolour comes in bottles with eyedropper applicators. There are many colours from which to choose: most good suppliers stock at least 60. However, a basic range of no more than 12 colours is more than adequate. It is better to experiment with mixing colours to achieve subtle shades than to increase the number of individual colours.

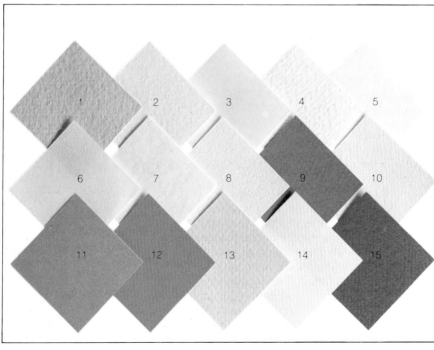

Watercolour paper
Some indication of the range of watercolour papers can be seen from these examples. Tinted papers are available, although it may be preferable to use white paper and apply a wash to make a background tint.
1. Greens de Wint Rugged
2. Crisbrook Hand-made
3. Kent
4. Arches M 38AM
5. Arches M 131AM
6. Rice M1140J
7. Schoellershammer T
8. Schoellershammer
9. Montgolfier
10. Montgolfier
11. Canson
12. Canson Fabriano
13. Canson Mi Teintes
14. Ingres
15. Ingres

Left *Tin Mine* This is an example of the use of watercolour without body colour. The white road markings and the left side of the building where it catches the light are areas of uncoloured paper. The right side of the building is represented by a very pale grey wash.

easier to achieve on a very rough surface, for example, if the paper is damp. Similar to damping the paper for stretching, it is not necessary to use a lot of water as the fibres can only absorb a certain amount. It should not be possible to see any water glistening on the surface, which occurs if too much has been applied; excess can always be sponged off. Use as large a brush as possible and fill it with the appropriate mixture of pigment and water. The board should be slightly tilted so that the paint will run. Lay the wash as quickly as possible, with broad strokes across the paper, starting at the top and working down. Try this also on a dry paper, with different quantities of water in the brush. If the paper has a very rough surface the colour may not penetrate all the pits in the surface, which result is called a "broken wash". When experimental washes have become controlled and even, the next step is to practise graduating them from top to bottom, and vice versa. The colour of a sky often changes very gradually towards the horizon. Blurred effects can be explored further by using more water than for a normal wash and floating colour onto it, or introducing a colour into an area of a different one before the first is dry. These soft effects have been much used in the treatment of skies.

The watercolourist, if he seeks to keep the painting as translucent as possible, works from light to dark. It is clearly important to make an early decision about the areas to be left absolutely white. If there are none at all then the colour closest in tone to white is established and this can be the first wash. If it is very pale it can be applied over the whole surface. The next darkest colour is then established and overlaid, and so on, until the very darkest at the end. One way of building up dark areas is to lay a wash over a colour which has already dried, but too many layers will eventually become dull. Turner and his contemporary, Thomas Girtin, adopted one method of expressing the shaded part of an object – painting the whole form with a pale wash, and then overpainting the dry shaded area with a darker mixture of the same colour.

The difficulties of working from light to dark will soon make themselves apparent. Some of the palest areas might be no more than tiny, intricate shapes, such as a cluster of leaves in bright sunlight, which will have to be carefully avoided when the darker surrounding washes are applied. If the colours are to remain transparent, it is not possible to make them

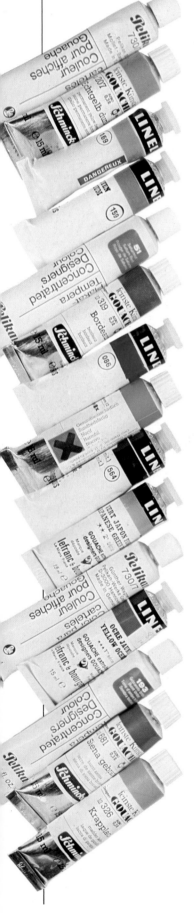

lighter again if the brush should accidentally slip. This is a problem inherent in the purist use of watercolour, which demands that as few corrections are made as possible.

The French called this approach the English method, but there have been many English watercolourists, including Paul Sandby, De Wint (1784-1849), Samuel Palmer (1805-81) and Turner, who used body colour as a way of making dark areas light again. The translucency prized by the purist is sacrificed, but a greater freedom is gained. Without white paint, the only way of making dark areas light is actually to remove the colour from the paper. There are several ways of doing this. Thomas Girtin wetted the offending colour again with a brush and then lifted it off with blotting paper. John Sell Cotman used dry bread. Others have scratched it off with a knife, but this can only be done when the paper is thick and strong. A more ingenious method of achieving light patches within a dark area, but one which requires forethought, is to make up a mixture of beeswax and turpentine with some flake white pigment, and paint it onto the light areas at the beginning. The darker wash can then be laid all over, the beeswax resisting the water in the wash. When the colour is dry the wax mixture is removed with turpentine, exposing the white paper underneath. The advantage of this is that the light areas can be painted as positive shapes, rather than having to work round them carefully with the darker colour.

Most watercolourists would accept it is desirable to use the white of the paper as far as possible, keeping a little white pigment in reserve which may be used only for tiny touches at the end. Other additions can be made with pen and ink. As there are limited opportunities for making radical alterations to a watercolour, an artist may turn in this way to other media, to rescue a work which might otherwise be considered to have failed. This medium can usefully be combined with chalk, pastel or with oil pastel to create different effects.

Pure watercolour is often at its best when completed swiftly and spontaneously. If serious mistakes are made early on it can be abandoned and started afresh on a clean piece of paper, and even the most skilful painter may attempt the same image several times before being satisfied. The other recourse is to let it develop into a gouache.

Gouache

Gouache is simply watercolour paint which has white added. Where watercolour is transparent, gouache is opaque. It can be bought in tubes or in jars, and is sometimes called "poster" colour. As the white of the paper is not used to lighten colours, it can be applied much more thickly. A larger range of brushes can be used as the pigment has more body than watercolour. With gouache the texture of the paint is important, but like watercolour it can be used in a very liquid state. To prevent the colours running together the drawing board should be fairly flat. As the colour dries it becomes lighter, and, if lighter than intended, it can be overpainted when the first colour is absolutely dry. The dry paint is very absorbent and can pick up dirt easily, so if fine detail is being added it is sensible to rest the painting hand on a clean piece of paper.

The qualities of gouache, its thick colour, opacity and its visible texture are quite different from watercolour. When both are used·together in the same picture, these differences can be exploited.

Tempera

Tempera is another form of watercolour, but instead of gum arabic either all or part of an egg was originally used to bind the pigment, and the paint called egg tempera. It was universally used for easel painting until the fourteenth and fifteenth centuries when it was combined with, and eventually superseded by, oil painting. It has been revived from time to time since then, and it is now possible to buy ready-made tempera colours. These colours are no longer made exclusively with egg, so the term tempera has come to cover emulsions of various sorts.

Tempera is an exacting medium, as the colours dry immediately and become paler. It is also very durable; the paint does not crack, discolour or deteriorate with changes of temperature or humidity. The oil in oil paint can attack and destroy the surface it is painted on, but tempera actually protects its support.

As with watercolour, tempera can be painted directly onto paper, but wood and canvas can also be used without a priming. Colours should be mixed on a non-absorbent palette similar to the watercolour palette; small china saucers or dishes are ideal. All sorts of brushes are suitable, but they should be

Right Tempera is usually produced by combining powdered pigments with an egg solution. The egg solution serves to bind the pigment to the surface. A limited range of colours are available ready mixed in the tube form, but these do not dry as readily as the handmade paint.

Making tempera
Tempera is a combination of egg binder and a pigment.
1. Crack an egg in half.

2. Separate the yolk from the white, allowing the white to drain away into a bowl.

3. Pick the yolk up very carefully, without breaking the sac.

washed frequently as the colour dries quickly.

This fast drying means that there is little scope for working the paint on the surface to create gradations. It has to be done instead by building up a gradual change of colour with tiny strokes of the brush, or cross-hatching. It is possible to buy preparations which retard the drying of the paint, but if these are used excessively it could be argued that they degrade the medium by depriving it of its own particular disciplines. However, such retarders have always been used; Filippo Lippi (c.1457-1504) used honey for this purpose.

To make the traditional egg tempera, mix pow-dered pigment thoroughly with egg yolk and allow it to dry. If scraped with a knife when dry it should have the consistency of candle wax. If it flakes, more pigment is needed. This is then moistened with water on a brush and applied to the paper or canvas. Colours can be made more transparent by including some white of egg.

It is not necessary to prime the canvas, but if a white surface is preferred, the primer can be made in the same way with white pigment, yolk of egg and water. To give the surface of a tempera painting a light gloss when it is finished it can be polished with silk, but the paint must be completely dry.

Above *Quay* This gouache explores the qualities of the medium with a great variety of greys. These have been enriched by areas of underpainting, made with transparent and semi-transparent washes of warm colour. In places these warm colours have been allowed to show through. The decorative qualities of the stones have been fully exploited.

4. Hold the yolk over a jar, slash the sac with a scalpel and let the yolk drain into the jar.

5. Add water to the yolk, a small amount at a time. The amount of water needed varies.

6. Make the pigment paste by first filling a small glass jar with pigment.

7. Add water to the pigment until it forms a thick paste. The amount required depends on the absorbency of the pigment.

8. Put the top on the jar and shake vigorously. Mix binder and paste together when required.

Garden in Richmond

watercolour on paper 20 x 23 inches (51 x 58 cm)

Although watercolour is a medium which can be used very quickly and spontaneously, there are occasions when the composition has to be carefully planned. In this example, the white of the paper is used for part of a sharply defined architectural detail, and it is important for the nature of the image that this shape remains a pure white. Before any colour was applied, the areas to be left white were covered with a masking fluid which could later be removed. This is a modern version of the beeswax and turpentine method used in the eighteenth century.

The white shapes where sunlight strikes the ornamental urn are the parts of the picture which initially hold our attention, but which subsequently lead us to the door in the wall behind. The link between the urn and the door is made by the association of architectural shapes, placed as they are among freely handled areas of trees and grass. Despite the prominence of the urn, the door is the real centre of attention. The colour of the door is the warmest colour in the painting, and the artist's intention is purely to play on our natural curiosity about what might lie on the other side of the wall.

burnt umber   cadmium red

chrome green

cobalt blue   Hooker's green

Payne's gray

ivory black   yellow ochre

1

2

3

4

5

6

7

8

The trees and grass are painted freely here, using several techniques which cannot be fully controlled. To preserve the clean shape of the garden urn it is first painted with masking fluid which protects the paper (1). Broad washes of cobalt blue and chrome green establish the sky and foreground (2) and the tree shapes are painted and blown to make spiky lines (3). The foliage is loosely washed in (4) and developed with blotted and spattered paint (5, 6) as the rigid shape of the wall is added. The mask is rubbed away and the urn drawn (7, 8).

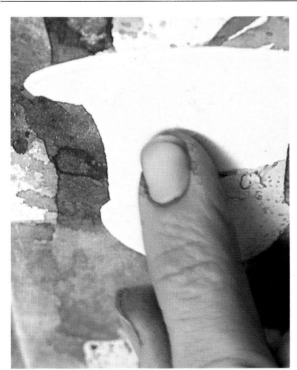

9

10

11

An inventive use of brushwork and less orthodox techniques give this painting a vibrant, textural quality enhanced by the emphatic highlight (9). The techniques fully exploit the transparency of watercolour. The texture of the foliage is made by adding loosely brushed and spattered colour, flicked from the end of the brush (10) to pools of green made by rolling a well-loaded brush over the paper. Crumpled tissue paper dabbed into wet paint (11) simulates a complex leafy pattern. All this can be freely applied over masking fluid, which is rubbed away to reveal the clean shape of the urn when the paint dries (12).

12

A Glastonbury Romance

watercolour on paper 20 x 12 inches (51 x 30 cm)

A broad sweep of landscape has an almost universal appeal. Most of us will go out of our way to enjoy a good view. City dwellers often find particular exhilaration in looking at wide open spaces and valleys such as the scene the artist has portrayed here. The complete absence of detail in the immediate foreground implies similar open spaces in the directions we cannot see, behind and to either side, as though we were alone in rolling countryside. All signs of human activity have been excluded from view, the scale of the valley and surrounding hills being given by the relative sizes of the trees as they diminish towards the distance. The considerable recession is achieved by using the very palest of colours for the hills on the horizon, with an alternation of warm and cool to take our eye back across the valley. It is a romantic view of nature, in the tradition of many English watercolourists since the eighteenth century.

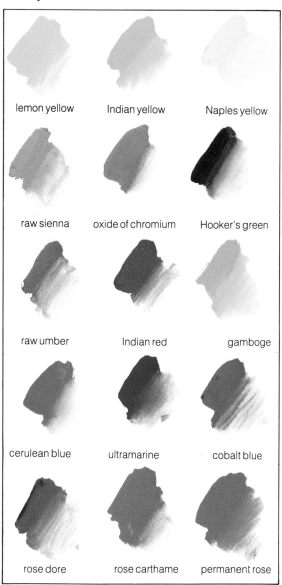

lemon yellow   Indian yellow   Naples yellow

raw sienna   oxide of chromium   Hooker's green

raw umber   Indian red   gamboge

cerulean blue   ultramarine   cobalt blue

rose dore   rose carthame   permanent rose

1

This painting demonstrates the classic watercolour technique of building from light to dark using thin washes of colour *(1)*. Heavy white paper is used as the support, stretched on a board so that it continues to dry flat as successive layers of wet paint are applied. The texture is varied by the use of various shapes and sizes of brushes, and by working wet into wet *(3)* or laying fresh colour over dried paint. As can be seen from the detail *(2)*, small dabs of paint dropped into a wet wash spread to give a fuzzy texture while hard-edged shapes are contrived by waiting until the broad areas are dry before detail is added.

3

4

2

5

The combination of wet washes of colour and small shapes which provide detail must be carefully controlled. Watercolour stains the paper and is not easily corrected. The choice of brush is important at each stage and a preference will gradually be found. A wide bristle brush (5) is useful for laying in heavy washes while round sable or pointed Chinese brushes are more suitable for details (4).

Watercolours are best mixed in a plastic or ceramic dish which must be white so the strength of the colour can be seen. As the colours lighten in drying the washes should be more intense than may appear necessary. This is a matter of judgement which develops finely with practice. In the first stage broad areas of colour are laid in to define different elements of land and sky (1). Here a central division of the picture plane is made with a line of green over a basic wash of cerulean blue, raw umber and indigo. The colour is laid very thinly. Wet colours are brushed into the wash and allowed to spread on either side of the centre line, giving the rough shape of the valley. As the paint dries the areas are given more emphasis (2), making use of the fuzziness of spreading colours and the runnels forming in the paper in which heavier tones collect. This can be useful in landscape painting, echoing the natural undulations of hills and valleys. As the basic forms emerge small dabs and strokes of raw umber, ultramarine and a mixture of the two are put in to show the lines of trees and hedges in the middle ground (3).

1

2

3

4

5

One dramatic sweep of a large bristle brush, well loaded with a mixture of Hooker's green and raw sienna, fills the foreground (4). The previous washes should be nearly dry so the line between foreground and middle ground is well defined, with a fairly hard edge. This largely alters the character of the work and gives a strong tone against which the other details can be emphasized. The horizon and sky are given a lighter tone by lifting paint with clean water and a sponge or dry brush. This must be done carefully or the paper surface may be damaged. Heavy tonal details are added to strengthen the hills in the middle distance on either side and a line of dark trees is put in to define the recession in the foreground (5). If the painting is allowed to dry the true tonal relationships can be seen and adjusted as necessary in the final stage.

Irish Hills

watercolour on paper 5 x 7 inches (13 x 18 cm)

Watercolour is a medium which is ideal for achieving very soft and gradual changes of tone and colour combined with a direct and spontaneous technique. Consequently, it is well suited to representing changing weather conditions, when clouds alter from one moment to the next; above all it is very suitable for rendering the watery skies of northern Europe. This painting exploits the appropriateness of the medium for the subject, evoking those days when dark rain clouds alternate with sudden and brief bursts of sunshine. It also shows the effectiveness of using a large brush loaded with water. This technique which produces unique drying marks, wholly consistent with the nature of the subject, when the water is absorbed by the paper.

The artist has made the weather and its effect on the landscape the main theme here, allowing the merging of sky and hills to fuse mysteriously. The pictorial space is created to some extent by the decreasing size of trees and fields, but more by atmospheric perspective, with warm colours in the foreground receding to cool blues and greys in the distance.

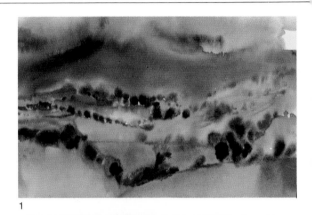

1

2

lemon yellow	Indian yellow	Naples yellow
raw sienna	oxide of chromium	Hooker's green
raw umber	Indian red	gamboge
cerulean blue	ultramarine	cobalt blue
rose dore	rose carthame	permanent rose

3

A sharp contrast of tone and colour is conveyed through a technique in which the blurring and soft interaction of wet watercolour washes suggest the forms (1, 2). The painting is atmospheric rather than fully descriptive and is created on a small scale which gives a certain vigour and tension to the marks. A soft Chinese brush is used (3) which has a thick base of hairs tapering to a very fine point.

4

5

Details of the painting show how fluid brushstrokes encourage the natural flow of the watery paint. Broad sweeps of colour laid with a round, soft brush melt together (4) and spread more readily if the paper is already dampened with clean water. Extra colour less heavily diluted can be dropped into the wash to vary the tonal qualities.

6

The colour can be lightly controlled or lifted by dabbing gently with an absorbent sponge or pad of tissue (5). This alters the tone and texture of the paint and also speeds up the painting process by removing excess moisture so colours can be overlaid more quickly. A medium-sized sable brush (6) is a good alternative to Chinese brushes for adding small details and precise shapes. It is vital to judge the drying time correctly so the colour diffuses just the right amount.

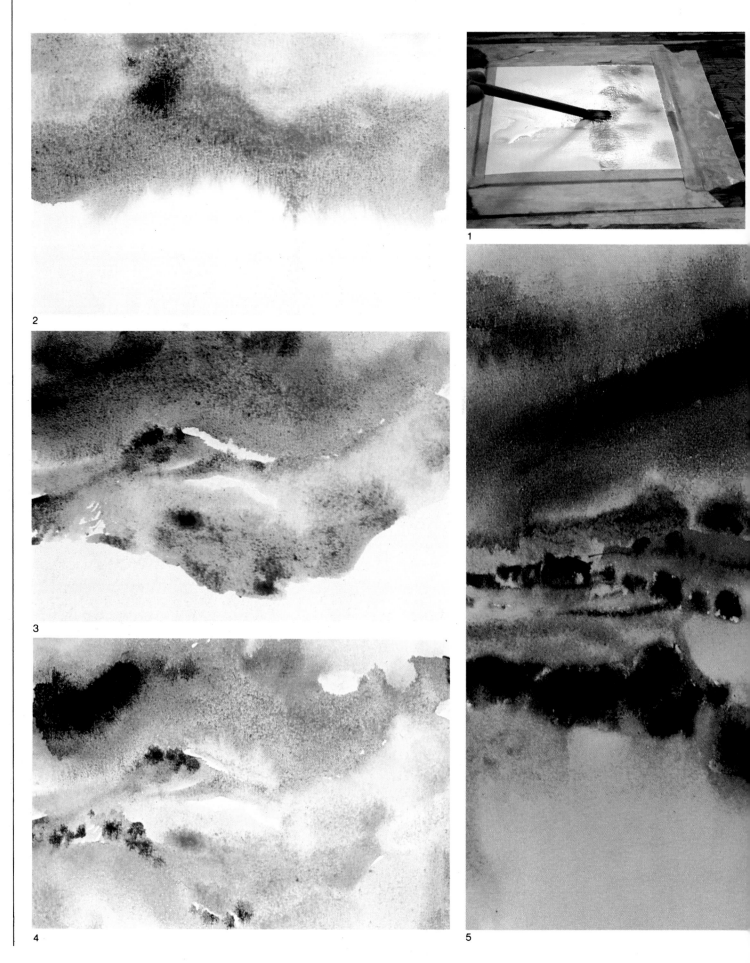

1

2

3

4

5

The painting has a well-defined colour scheme, divided between the heavy blue of the mountain and the yellow tones in the foreground, linked by warm pink and grey washes and the dark lines of trees and bushes. The dark band of blue is established immediately (1), merging gently into a wash of blue and rose suggesting the sky. These colours are put down with plenty of water (2) so the blue spreads and flows naturally, drying without harsh lines at either edge. The mauve-pink is extended into the foreground (3) and small patches of strong green and yellow are laid in which follow the rhythm of the gently curving landscape below the mountain. The colours are mixed to form subtle greys which shade and deepen the brighter hues. Well-judged control of the moisture is essential. The painting need not dry out completely at any stage but if it is too wet the colours will simply mix and become muddy. Details of the trees are gradually developed with dark green and raw umber (4) carefully placed in small dabs and patches. The tones are extended and enriched throughout the image. Contrasts are built up more heavily in the final stage (5) with the colours brushed in and blotted to create form and space. To give a misty effect around the mountains and sky a little white is dropped into the colour washes, making the paint slightly opaque.

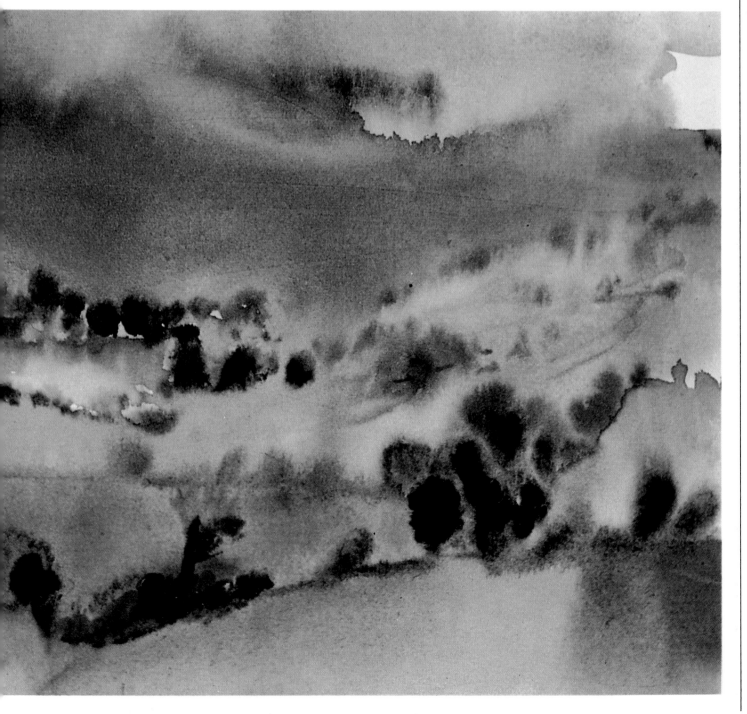

Above *Trees in Spring*
A fresh and spontaneous watercolour which exploits the white of the paper to express bright sunshine. The large trees in the background are seen against the light, which enables the artist to contrast the variety of tones found in the smaller tree in front of them. The different types of trees and plants are expressively and economically conveyed by a variety of brushstrokes.

Summer Painting

watercolour on paper 9½ x 13 inches (24 x 33 cm)

In this work the artist was interested in the ways in which a landscape changes, sometimes dramatically, from season to season and under different weather conditions. Although the fields and hills are firmly established in space, it is not the artist's intention that we should see them separately from the low clouds that transform them. The transparency of watercolour has been used in varying degrees to achieve this.

The spontaneity which is so effective in this medium imposes considerable disciplines on the artist. To capture transitory cloud effects, in the manner we see here, involves working at great speed while judging the correct proportions of pigment and water, and getting it right first time. There are some ways that mistakes can be rectified, but for pale and delicate passages, such as thin watery clouds, the work can quickly look laboured and lack freshness if not applied swiftly and confidently.

Here the artist has observed the soft and subtle gradation of tone that give the scene its atmosphere. The stronger greens in the foreground ensure that we appreciate the scale of the whole landscape.

To capture the effects of light with brush and pigment is an extremely difficult task. In this subject (1) there is a combination of the brightness of summer light and the heavy atmosphere created in a passing shower. Watercolour is the perfect medium for this task as its rich, translucent hues and subtle tonal mixtures have the delicacy necessary for an effective rendering. Again the basic areas of colour are built up in broad washes of thin paint (2) and details added with accurately placed patches of tone and colour (3). As the landscape takes shape the brushstrokes become all-important, especially in the final stages where broad bands of grey are laid over the colours to create the atmospheric effect of the rain clouds. This layering technique suggests the shroud of mist and rain through which the summer light still breaks.

1

2

3

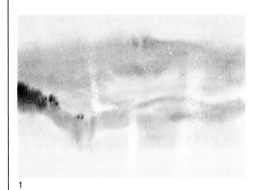

1

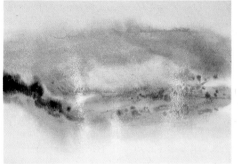

2

3

The work is laid flat *(above)* to prevent the colours from running uncontrollably and to give free access to the painting. The brushwork should be loose and confident, giving a vigorous rhythm to the washes of colour and lines of detail. As the tones gradually build up the diffused colours form a web of shapes and hues which are drawn out by adding definition with the point of the brush *(right)*. Many colours are allowed to mix on the paper to achieve the full effect.

In the early stages the colours are deliberately allowed to blur and merge together, mixing into subtle tones which suggest the division between sky and land. The paper is wetted with clean water and blue, green and yellow washes laid in, with a slightly darker emphasis added in raw umber on the lefthand side *(1)*. As the colours dry a warm pink tone is brushed into the sky and touches of blue in the middle ground *(2)*. The foreground is blocked in with a broad bristle brush, the paint still kept wet so that it dries in a mass of uneven tone *(3)*. More detail is added in the middle ground with green and brown mixtures. The sky is given a yellow cast to represent light breaking through the cloud and this is overlaid with diagonal strokes of blue-grey *(4)*. These are made more emphatic and merged into the blues in the landscape *(5)*. Colours in the foreground are strengthened *(6)* and the stormy sky given an opaque grey cast by adding a little white to the paint *(7)*.

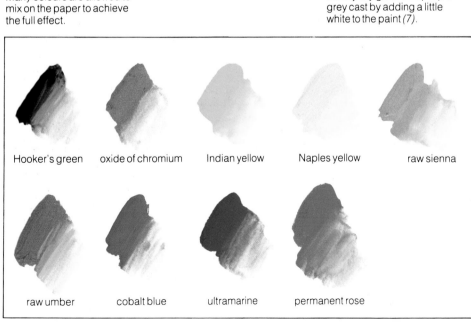

Hooker's green   oxide of chromium   Indian yellow   Naples yellow   raw sienna

raw umber   cobalt blue   ultramarine   permanent rose

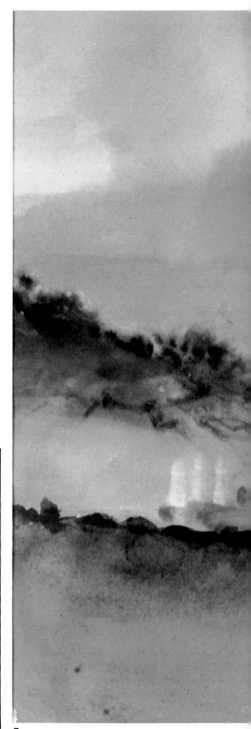

7

4

5

6

Oil and Acrylic

The use of pigments ground with vegetable oils has ancient origins, but was not adopted and developed by artists until the beginning of the fifteenth century. Most large scale pictures and decorations before then were executed in mosaic or fresco, but these techniques demanded the cooperation of a team of craftsmen and their apprentices. Smaller works were done with various forms of watercolour and egg tempera, none of which permitted much reworking. The limitations of these techniques, combined with an increasing desire among artists to express a more personal vision, prompted the development of a freer, more flexible painting medium.

Oil had earlier been used as a final glaze on tempera, which always dries quickly and becomes lighter as it dries. These glazes gave the tempera surface an added richness and helped to unify the colours. This practice continued up to the time of Rubens, when many painters were adopting oil as the dominant medium. Jan and Hubert van Eyck, fifteenth century painters who lived in Bruges, and Giovanni Bellini (c.1430/40-1516) from Venice, are commonly acknowledged to have made the most important innovations in oil painting techniques, although south of the Alps the change from tempera was more gradual. The paintings by the van Eyck family are well preserved because they took great pains in the preparation of their materials.

There have been technical developments since the innovatory period but these have mostly been concerned with making the handling of oil paint as free as possible. While this freedom from the disciplines imposed by tempera, watercolour, fresco, pastel or mosaic makes oil easier to use in some ways, it also demands a great number of difficult choices and decisions. Most shops selling artists' materials have overwhelming displays of colours, brushes, solvents, canvases, boards, varnishes, and primers. Restraint should be practised from the start; much can be achieved with the simplest equipment. Tempera and watercolour impose inherent disciplines, but oil requires the artist to impose his own.

The oil used in the manufacture of oil paint is either linseed or, particularly in France, poppy. It is now rare for an artist to make his own oil paints, but when this was common practice there was an opportunity to control the qualities of each colour. Different

Left Oil paints are best bought individually. To begin with, it is wise to use a small range of colours; other colours can be made by mixing. A good basic palette for a beginner would be: titanium white; a yellow, such as yellow ochre, lemon yellow or Naples yellow; cadmium orange; baryta green (emerald), viridian green or terre verte; cerulean and cobalt blue and ultramarine; a red, such as alizarin crimson, cadmium red or Venetian red; a brown, such as burnt umber, raw umber or burnt sienna; cobalt violet or mars violet; ivory black, lamp or vine black.

Above Mixing basic oil paint with oil or a thinner such as turpentine allows the artist to control certain properties: thickness of the paint, drying time and texture are among the variables.

Right There are many oil painting sets on the market. Look for one with a good selection of colours and good quality brushes. This kit contains a palette, palette knife, oil, varnish and turpentine.

Making oil paint
1. Spoon powdered pigment onto a glass slab and pour enough oil onto it to make a thick mixture.

2. Blend the oil and pigment using a spatula.

3. Mix the pigment with the oil using a glass muller. Press down firmly and move the muller in circles.

4. Store the paint in a glass jar. Cover with a little water if it is to be kept for long.

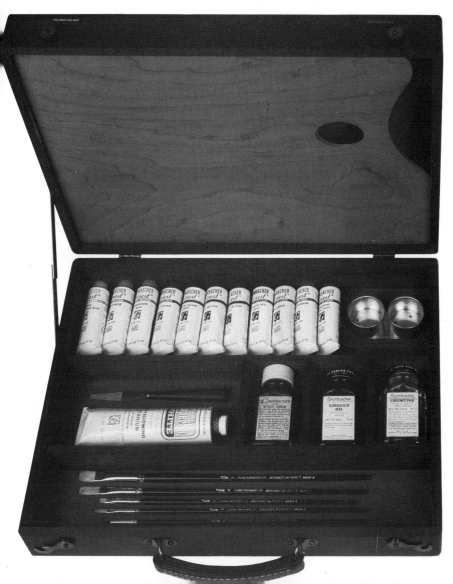

pigments absorb different amounts of oil, just as different quantities of gum arabic are needed in the preparation of watercolours. Oil colours are now bought in tubes, and unfortunately manufacturers must consider such problems as the shelf-life of their product, which sometimes results in the addition of more oil than necessary. The control which is now possible is only the result of long experience of each colour's drying time, transparency, permanence and viscosity, and its reaction to further additions of oil. A faithful copy of a painting made before the introduction of paint in tubes would now be impossible, as we no longer have the degree of control over the medium as the artists who made up their own pigments for a specific requirement.

A technical point which is easy to overlook when working, is that if a colour is painted on top of another, the first coat should be absolutely dry. There is a danger of the paint eventually cracking if this is not observed. It is even more important if there is more oil in the first colour than in the second. If the artist likes to paint with more oil than a colour contains in the tube, he can add more, but it is safer to reserve this practice for the latter stages of the picture. If the paint needs to be looser or more liquid early on, this should be achieved by adding turpentine rather than oil. A hazard of using too much oil, at any stage, is a tendency for the surface to wrinkle when it dries. This is because the oil expands as it is exposed to air. There is no way to avoid this except by using it with moderation. It is always advisable to keep the extra oil stored in the light, because in the dark the oil becomes dark.

There are few painters who use nothing but oil to dilute and liquefy their colours. Most use turpentine, often to the exclusion of additional oil altogether. Genuine turpentine should be used, rather than substitutes such as white spirit, which may be used for cleaning brushes and palettes but is not suitable as a paint thinner.

Colours

The properties of oil colours, their permanence and their ability to mix with others, are constantly under research. It is sad to see traditional pigments becoming rare and expensive, but new and often more stable alternatives appear all the time. Artists' colours are made from a wide range of materials, varying from dead beetles and the urine of yaks fed on mangoes, to complicated chemical mixtures. There is no need to know the origins of a pigment, but it is a good idea to ascertain its permanence and mixing ability.

The beginner will learn most by confining himself to as small a palette as possible. A basic palette might consist of titanium white, yellow ochre, light red, cobalt blue and black. Other colours can be made by mixing; in this way, the beginner learns the potentialities of each pigment. The only exception to this rule is when an artist places brilliance of colour above all else, as a colour made by mixing several will be slightly denser, and less light will reflect through it from the white surface on which it is laid. A palette can always be extended later.

A toxic label should not deter the use of certain pigments, as this would eliminate too many essential colours. Normal precautions should be taken, such as keeping paints away from young children and not chewing on brushes in moments of stress.

It is worth remembering that one of the greatest colourists, Titian, used a very limited palette. He is reported to have said that only three colours are necessary. In theory, any colour should be obtainable from the three primary colours, red, yellow and blue, but in practice this only works with absolutely pure pigments which are not available as artists' paints. Titian did not even have the use of a bright yellow, a pigment developed well after his time, and he made do with yellow ochre; but he did have genuine ultramarine and madder, with the addition of a few earth colours.

Rather than using black it is nearly always worth mixing dark colours, as this stimulates the eye to perceive the real nature of shadows. Very dark greys can be obtained by mixing blue with either raw umber or burnt sienna; black should only be used as a last resort if these mixtures are still not dark enough. It is easy to make a colour darker by simply adding black, but if this is done too much the result will be dull. Reasons such as this will be found to justify extending the suggested five-colour palette. Here is a possible nine-colour palette: flake white, lemon yellow, yellow ochre, cadmium red, Indian red, raw umber, burnt sienna, viridian green and cobalt blue. This selection provides the potential for many variations.

Flake white can be replaced by, or used in addition to, titanium white. The latter is denser and occasionally necessary for its ability to cover a darker colour. The yellows, reds and browns are included as warm and cool counterparts. Cadmium yellow, pale, vivid or deep, could replace the lemon. Yellow ochre is always useful. A brighter cool red could be alizarin crimson or rose madder. Burnt umber could be added as a warm version of raw umber. Ultramarine is a useful additional blue.

Before starting to paint from nature, it is useful to experiment with mixing pigments. Rather than assuming that grey is simply a combination of black and white, it is better to try combinations like white, viridian and Indian red, or cobalt and raw umber, or ultramarine and burnt sienna. Different combinations of blues and yellows produce a wide range of greens. Landscape painters often also need to use a variety of soft, delicate tones.

Above right *Hampshire Lane* The composition is arranged so that the spectator's eye will follow the twist and dip in the country road. There is a concentration of small shapes where the shadows of tree trunks fall across the road, leading the eye to the white fence in the middle distance.

Right *The Grounds of the Château Noir,* Cézanne. Where the Impressionists concentrated on visual sensations of light, Cézanne's priority was the structural content of his motif. This painting owes its strength to the fine tension between the structure of the trees' forms and the carefully composed pattern on the surface on the canvas.

Supports

The support is the name given to the material onto which the paints are applied. It can be wood, paper, hardboard, canvas or even metal. For oil painting, canvas or hardboard are most commonly used. Wooden panels must be well seasoned, which is now rare, and their weight makes them less suitable for the landscape painter. A good quality paper is a possibility, but it needs to be clipped to a similarly awkward board and, if the paint is applied thickly, it would probably need permanent reinforcement at the back. Cardboard is a better support, but has the disadvantage of being made of poor quality materials which become brittle with time. There are various cards and boards made specially for artists, but these are sold with prepared surfaces which make them expensive. Hardboard is a firm, strong, durable material but the back has a coarser surface with a deep grain imposed by the machine on which it was made. It is ugly and mechanical and should never be used for painting. The front is more suitable, but it needs to be rubbed with a medium sandpaper to remove the shine.

Canvas certainly has the most advantages. It is light, it can be bought in a great variety of weaves, and is universally available either in its natural state or already prepared for painting. It can be rolled up when the painting is finished and dry. Linen makes the best canvas. Cotton is not strong enough and is too elastic. Those who wish to buy unprepared canvas should first stretch it. If time is available, this gives the artist an opportunity to obtain the particular sort of surface he likes best. The nature of the surface is often the most important factor in the choice of support.

Wooden stretchers for canvas can be bought in almost any length and have ends which are mitred and slotted, which enable the artist to tighten the canvas if it stretches and sags. When slotting two sides together make sure that all the bevels are at the front, to prevent the wood from touching the canvas when in use, causing ridges. The four corners should be knocked tightly together, forming perfect right-angles. This is best done by measuring the diagonals of the rectangle until they are the same. If the canvas is large, there should be an extra cross piece between the longest two sides, to support them when the canvas shrinks during preparation. A shrinking canvas exerts a surprising force. Any size larger than about 30 x 40 inches (approximately 80 x 100 cm) should have this strut if the canvas is not primed.

Above *Types of canvas*
1. Unbleached calico is inexpensive.
2. Cotton canvas is a cheaper alternative to linen.
3. Hessian is coarse.
4, 5. Linen makes the best canvas and comes in different weaves.
6. Primed linen is suitable for most purposes.

Left *Yuba County* This English painter's view of northern California shows his enjoyment of a relatively new range of landscape colours, but it is interesting that this has not prompted him to buy tubes of colour that he does not normally use. Instead, he has made new mixtures from his customary palette, which is surprisingly limited, considering the great variety of soft greens, ochres and umbers with which he has composed this picture.

When the stretcher has been fitted together and forms a perfect rectangle, lay it onto the canvas, which should be 2 inches (5 cm) with the bevelled edges downwards. The canvas weave should be parallel to the stretcher sides. Fold the canvas round to the back and fasten it in the middle of one side with a large-headed tack or staple, then pull the canvas taut across and fasten it directly opposite on the other side. Do the same on the other two sides, then, pulling the canvas tight, move along towards each corner, fixing at opposite sides as you go. It is better to work evenly out to the corners, keeping each side in step with the others, rather than fastening the canvas completely on one side before doing the next, as this stretches the canvas unevenly. When all the sides are fixed, lift up the corners of the canvas and lay them on the line of the mitre, leaving two loose pockets at either side to be tucked in as neatly as possible. Take care not to put a tack through the ends of the stretchers, which makes it impossible to tighten the canvas later on. Tightening is achieved with small wooden wedges which should be supplied with the stretcher. They fit into slots on the inside of each corner, and should be used as equally as possible at each corner or the canvas will cease to be rectangular. It is not always necessary to use them, especially on small works, but a canvas will stretch with the constant action of the brush. The wedges enable the artist to keep the canvas taut.

Grounds

Whatever material is used for the support, its surface must be prepared with a ground or primer. The preparation of canvas for oil painting should achieve two aims. The first is to protect it from the oil in the paint. Oil will oxidize in time and become acid, and when this happens the canvas cannot survive for long. The second is to provide a surface which the painter finds most suitable for working on. The absorbency of this surface can vary according to taste. It does not have to be white, but white will minimize any tendency of the colours to darken over long periods.

Preparation of the canvas is easier when it is already on the stretcher, but is important to allow for the shrinkage which will take place by not having the canvas too taut. Fingers are normally strong enough for tightening the canvas on the stretcher; canvas pliers are available but generally unnecessary. Preferably, however, the canvas is prepared before it is stretched, to avoid any distortion of the stretcher or the canvas as it shrinks.

The first stage of priming, or laying a ground on a canvas, is to apply a thin coat of glue size, preferably rabbit skin glue. Size, bought in small thin sheets or crystals, should be dissolved in enough water to cover the canvas. It is difficult to give exact measures, but if it is in crystal form use about one tablespoon to half a pint (.3 l) of water. Heat the water in a pan and stir in the size until completely dissolved. The water must not be allowed to boil. One way of testing the strength is to put a drop of warm size on a finger and as it cools press the finger and thumb together. It should be-

Right *Early morning, San Francisco* The magnificent sunrises and sunsets of Turner and Claude have inhibited many artists from approaching these subjects but thoughtful observation puts nothing out of bounds. There has been no exaggeration here of the colours we normally associate with sunrise, and no over-dramatization. The artist has concentrated on the organization of his composition so that we can understand the spaces he has chosen to depict, rather than making any more of the sky and its limitless distances than we can actually see. The link of orange between the sky and the foreground directs us to observe the effects of light on the immediate environment at this time of day.

Stretching a canvas
1. You will need a ruler, knife, staple gun and staples and a pair of canvas pliers.

2. Fit the corners of the stretcher together. Tap each corner with a hammer to make sure that they fit securely.

3. Measure the diagonals to make sure that the stretcher is perfectly square.

come sticky but not too sticky. The size must not be too strong or it will eventually crack when painted over.

Apply the warm size with a large flat decorator's brush, covering even the edges. Surfaces other than canvas may be more absorbent and require two thin coats. It should be left to dry overnight.

The next stage is the white priming. Recently, paint manufacturers have produced an efficient ready-to-use primer based on titanium oxide. This is a dense white which is very stable. It can be used on all surfaces which have been sized, and is suitable for both oil and acrylic painting. Some painters prefer to make their own grounds so they can control the absorbency. There are many recipes, but a simple general purpose ground can be made by mixing zinc white with yolk of egg and water. It dries very quickly and subsequent coats can be applied without too long a delay. This is clearly less convenient than the readymade grounds, which are worth trying out before making one's own. Their only disadvantage seems to be that they become hard if kept in a shop too long. It is wise to open a tin before buying it to make sure it is still liquid, and buy no more than is needed. If necessary, it can be diluted a little with turpentine.

All grounds should be applied in at least two coats. Each coat should be thin, and thoroughly dry before the next is laid. Again a large flat brush is used and each coat applied as evenly as possible. The roughness, or "tooth", of the surface can be controlled to some extent when the final layer of the ground is applied. For a rough surface the primer can be lightly stippled with the end of the brush as it begins to dry. A smooth surface can be obtained by rubbing the last coat gently with fine sandpaper. This should be done without rubbing through to the canvas.

Many will prefer to buy canvas or board which is already stretched and primed. This can be expensive and, although different qualities are generally available, ready primed canvas is not absorbent enough for some tastes. Little can be done to remedy this. If on the other hand a ground is too absorbent, whether bought or prepared by the artist himself, the surface can be covered with a thin coat of retouching varnish. Always make sure, throughout the preparation of a canvas, that each coat is completely dry before any

4. Allow 1½ inches (3.5 cm) overlap all around. Cut the canvas using a knife and ruler.

5. Place the stretcher on the canvas. Pull the canvas around at one end and staple on the outer edge of the stretcher.

6. Pull the canvas taut at the opposite end and staple. Repeat for the other two sides.

7. Staple at intervals of 3 inches (7.5 cm), up to 2 inches (5 cm) at the corners. Fold in the corners.

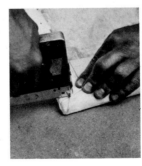

8. Secure the corners with two staples each.

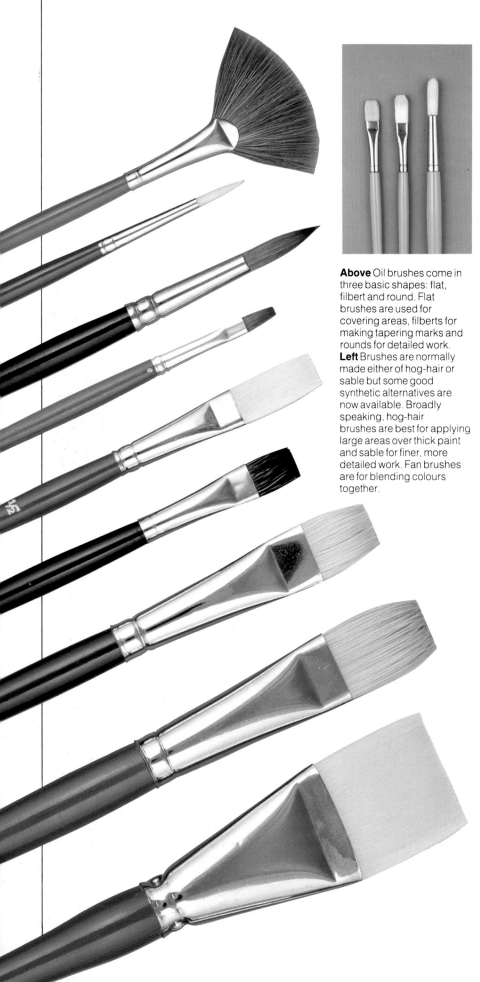

Above Oil brushes come in three basic shapes: flat, filbert and round. Flat brushes are used for covering areas, filberts for making tapering marks and rounds for detailed work.
Left Brushes are normally made either of hog-hair or sable but some good synthetic alternatives are now available. Broadly speaking, hog-hair brushes are best for applying large areas over thick paint and sable for finer, more detailed work. Fan brushes are for blending colours together.

subsequent coat is applied, and before the painting is started.

Equipment

Brushes Brushes come in so many shapes and sizes that it is difficult to make any positive recommendations except to say that they must be of the best quality. The shape and size to suit each artist can only be discovered by trial and error. Brushes are normally made either of hog-hair or of sable. Hog-hair brushes have a stiff bristle and can be bought in larger sizes than sable. They are more suitable if the paint is to be applied thickly, or if the paint is used straight from the tube without being thinned with turpentine. Sables are more appropriate if the paint surface is to be kept smooth, and when very fine detail is required. Both hog-hair and sable brushes are made in three main shapes: flat, which has bristles of the same length and a square end; filbert, which is flat with the bristles arranged to form a rounded end; and round, with bristles set in a tubular ferrule tapering to a rounded end. Four different sizes of "rounds" made of hog-hair between no.1 (the smallest) and no.8 would be quite sufficient to start with, perhaps adding a small sable for very fine detail. Brushes for oil painting have longer handles than watercolour brushes, which permit the painter to hold them in different ways and to work at a greater distance from his canvas. This is often desirable when a canvas is large.

Some brushes, particularly hog-hair, wear down quickly, and grounds with much tooth tend to accelerate the wear, so it is worth buying brushes with long bristles. After use they should be cleaned every day before the paint has hardened, or the bristles will splay into a useless shape. The most thorough way to clean them is with soapy water in the palm of the hand, making sure that the paint is removed up to the ferrule. When clean they should be drawn back into shape. While you are painting they can be cleaned, preferably with white spirit as turpentine is oily and can gum the bristles together.

The paintbox This is a useful item for the landscape painter, although not indispensable. It should be no larger than necessary, but it is best to have one which will hold as much of the equipment as possible. The most suitable boxes are divided into compartments which hold the contents in place. There should be a separate compartment, the length of the box, for brushes. Make sure that this is long enough to hold the longest brush; it is annoying to buy a brush and find it has to be carried separately. There should be room for bottles of oil, turpentine and possibly white spirit. A dipper, a little metal container for oil or turpentine, is also useful. The best dippers have a screw top which keep the medium in good condition when not actually being used. (Turpentine should not be exposed to light and air longer than necessary.) An extra dipper should be carried for cleaning the brushes. Varnishes need not be carried as it is unlikely that a painting will be dry enough before it is brought home for varnish to be applied.

A paintbox large enough to hold all this equipment

Above *Evening, Clodmore Hill* This painting evokes the emotive value of large areas of bright colour earlier explored by Gauguin. It is also in line with a more specifically English tradition which stems from the early pastoral landscapes of Samuel Palmer, which were very romantic and mystical.

Left *Greek Landscape* A symmetrical placing in the foreground of the house and two olive trees creates a firm composition which is given more point by the touches of light catching the jagged cliffs behind. There is also a fine balance between the use of local colours and the way in which they are modified by the evening light.

will also be able to hold a palette of a reasonable size. Many boxes are made to hold a rectangular palette in the lid. The palette can be plastic, or wooden, which would be easy to make. Plywood is adequate, but the surface must be treated to reduce its absorbency by rubbing it with beeswax dissolved in turpentine until it has a good, smooth finish. A palette knife is useful for scraping unwanted paint from the palette, and for mixing colours in large quantities. Any spare space in the box should be filled with cotton rags which are essential for cleaning brushes and the palette while working, and also for wiping paint off the canvas.

The easel The only other piece of essential equipment is the easel. There are many on the market which are light and fold into a small space. Some are flimsy, and some can hold only small canvases. Strength and stability are important, although a strong wind can capsize even the sturdiest. In this situation, the strength of an easel would enable the painter to suspend stones or pieces of wood from a central point so anchoring it in position.

Few portable easels are made with sufficiently long legs to permit the artist to work standing up. This is unfortunate for those who like to stand back from their work at frequent intervals. A collapsible stool will also be needed.

An alternative to carrying a separate paintbox and easel is a contrivance which combines both. This has the advantage of being easier to carry, and means that the easel itself will be sturdier.

Techniques

When painting directly from nature, it is worth remembering not to attempt too much detail, and to concentrate on the accurate observation of colour relationships. It is easy to make bright colours too bright, and not consider how they are modified by the prevailing light. This is generally the result of looking at a colour in isolation. It is helpful, when beginning a painting, to put as many of the observed colours on the canvas as quickly as possible, so that the value of each can be assessed in relation to the others.

The early marks on the canvas should be kept as thin as possible. As layers are painted one on another, they can be increasingly oilier, but an oily first layer will cause the paint to crack. The brushmarks may look ugly if later painted over with a thinner colour, and sometimes even contradict the purpose of the second colour.

An alternative to modifying a colour by repainting is to apply a second colour with broken brushstrokes, so that the first colour shows through. This is called "scumbling" and is also used by pastellists, who cannot mix their pigments to the same extent as painters. Another technique for modifying an existing colour is "glazing". This is the application of a layer of paint which has been considerably thinned with oil over a more opaque one. It is more properly a studio technique as it involves waiting for layers to dry, but it can produce rich effects.

If the paint is worked a lot, and many alterations are made, some areas of the painting will go dead and colours will lose their natural value and brilliance. Retouching varnish can be used to restore a colour's brilliance by reducing its absorbency. It is a quick-drying varnish, which must only be used when the "dead" paint is dry. It should be applied as thinly as possible; just enough to fill the pores in the paint. Some artists prefer to mix a little ordinary varnish with their oil or turpentine at the outset, to make such retouching unnecessary and to accelerate the drying of the paint. For this purpose there are three main varieties available, Copal, Mastic and Damar, but it is better to keep the painting fresh without taking such measures.

Even when the painting is finished, it is not essential to varnish it, but there may be some slightly duller parts which were not retouched while the work was in progress. In this case a thin film of retouching varnish can be applied all over the painting, or one of the above can be applied if an increased brilliance or a heavier protection is thought necessary. Mastic or Damar are considered safer than Copal, which is virtually impossible to remove should this ever be necessary.

Liquid varnishes should be applied with the painting laid flat, with a soft brush, in a dry, dust-free atmosphere, as swiftly and evenly as possible, without going over the same place twice. If a high gloss is

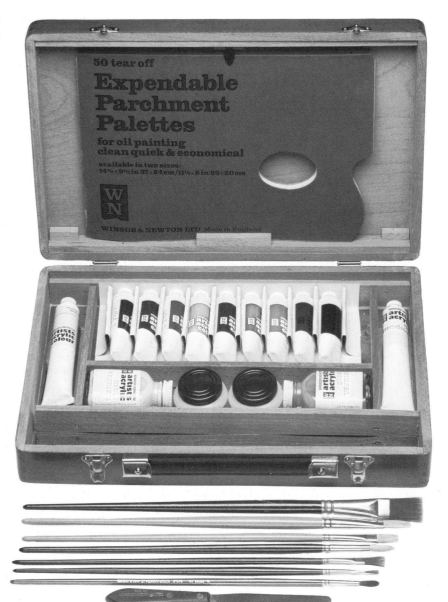

Above Acrylic paints, like oils, are available in sets from a number of manufacturers. Basic equipment should include a selection of colours similar to the range for oils, a palette, mixing dishes and several brushes. The best brushes for acrylic paints are the synthetic ones specially developed for this use. Sable or hog-hair brushes can also be used. Because acrylic paint is extremely quick-drying, all painting equipment must be cleaned immediately after use. This is particularly important for brushes.

not desirable, there are some efficient wax varnishes available, which bring out the colours, provide ample protection, and can either be left with a matt surface or polished to give a little shine.

Acrylic

Acrylic paints have been shown to be a sound and flexible new development. They use water as a medium rather than oil. They dry extremely quickly, so there are none of the worries about overpainting which concern the oil painter, and they provide a suitable medium for working at great speed. They can be thinned with plenty of water and blown onto the canvas with a spray. The surface on which they are applied can be cut up and moulded with no risk of the paint cracking, unless it is very thick, which makes them suitable for collage. It is also possible to use them as a thin, quick-drying undercoat for oil painting, although they cannot be put on top.

Despite their flexibility, acrylics do have some disadvantages. Brushes must be washed thoroughly in lots of water at frequent intervals, and there is a

danger of paint drying on the palette before it is even used. For this reason the less absorbent the palette the better. A plastic one, or even a piece of glass is preferable to a wooden palette. The paints can also darken noticeably as they dry, especially if thinned with water. The technology of acrylic paint has only been developed in the last 20 years, and there are enormous differences between different makes, the less good ones drying more quickly than the better. It is a good idea to keep tubes of acrylic paint in a tightly sealed plastic box in order to minimize this drying. There are an increasing number of additives which give greater control, such as drying retarders and "tension breakers" which alter their viscosity.

Acrylic paints have less body than oil paints, and are well suited to smooth flat areas. Their opacity is very similar from one colour to another, unlike the variations found in oil pigments. Some would consider this an advantage and others the loss of an appealing dimension. One undeniable advantage of acrylics is that they can be applied to any surface without priming.

Above *A Haystack* (1978–79), William Delafield Cook. This Australian painter uses photography for his work in a deliberate and sophisticated way. He takes photographs of his chosen motif, making sure to achieve a high technical quality. These photographs are a series of prints of every small section of the scene, so that he has the maximum amount of detailed information. All the prints are then joined together to cover the whole area included in the compositions. The painting is then built up in many stages, using very fine brushwork. The rapid drying time of acrylics enables the artist to develop an area with an infinite number of tiny strokes.

Right Acrylic paint is available in tubes or in pots. Various media can be added to acrylic paint to increase the range of effects and techniques. These include gloss, texture paste and polymer medium to add body. It is best to use these with care.

The Track: Autumn

oil on canvas 30 x 30 inches (76 x 76 cm)

This study of a landscape in late autumn and the snow scene on the following pages were both painted from approximately the same position. A comparison of the two shows how an artist might approach the same subject in a variety of ways according to exactly what his eye is presented with on each occasion. The colours in a landscape and the way in which the light affects them may change radically, and this happens not only from one season to another but also at different times on the same day. An accent of colour visible at one time may attract the eye as a natural focal point and consequently prompt a composition which will exploit this feature. At other times this accent may seem unimportant.

The autumn landscape was painted in overcast weather, with a heavy, dull sky and no direct sunlight. These conditions tend to make colours flat. The artist chose to concentrate on a small section of the scene so that the composition arose more from the angles and directions found in the forms of the landscape than from, for example, a pattern of shadows. One result of this decision was that distant features, such as the cottage among the trees, were in danger of seeming closer than they were in reality, so the track in the foreground assumed a particular importance as a means of establishing the space between the spectator and the middle distance. The track also creates large triangles in the foreground which offset the verticals of the trees and the horizontals of the middle distance.

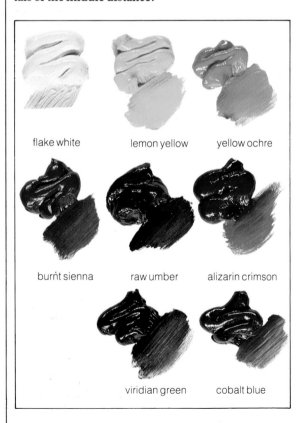

flake white

lemon yellow

yellow ochre

burnt sienna

raw umber

alizarin crimson

viridian green

cobalt blue

1

2

3

4

5

It is not always necessary to draw up a composition in detail before painting. In landscape particularly, the effect often depends upon colours and masses which are best approached directly. However, a few lines brushed in lightly with a grey or neutral tone are valuable for establishing the main features of the landscape *(1)*. Continuing with brown and grey tones small areas of easily identifiable colour are loosely brushed in. It is useful to block in broad areas of colour as quickly as possible *(2)* which lay the basis for a more detailed analysis of the shapes and tones. Here the warm (brown) and cool (blue-grey) tones are blocked in. These are developed with the addition of local colour *(3)*, such as the green of the grassy track and the heavy shape of the dark brown tree. At the same time the linear design of the composition is emphasized in more detail, with fine brushmarks describing the distant trees. As colour and texture are built up the sense of distance is preserved by using the richest colours in the foreground and reworking the misty blue and mauve tones of the horizon line *(4)*. In the finished work *(5)* the focal points are brought out with tonal contrasts and detailed drawing with the brush.

The Track: Winter

oil on canvas 20 x 28 inches (51 x 71 cm)

In this snow scene, an extremely different perspective was adopted. The forms of the landscape were defined almost solely by the blue shadows. In the autumn picture, the track was made into an important element in the composition because it led the eye into the landscape at the same time as providing a strong colour change between the stubble of the field and the green grass where tractors had driven. But after a heavy fall of snow the only indications of the track's position were the small shadows cast by the furrows left by the last wheels that went along it. The local colour of the grass has been replaced by a surface reflecting chance conditions of light.

One of the artist's aims in this painting was to convey, the extreme brightness of the snow, so the colours were kept in a high key. In conditions of bright sunlight on snow, local colours are almost entirely absent, so the balance between light and dark, and sunlight and shade, is of critical importance. If the shadows are made too dark there is a danger of distorting the surface of the field. If too light, the brightness of the illuminated areas will lose its force.

A landscape covered with snow offers an artist a unique opportunity to observe its forms in a truly sculptural way, without the attractions and distractions that the normal colours may provide. At the same time, this absence of a variety of colour means that the smallest clues which suggest the shape of the landscape must be exploited to the full. A tree's shadow may be the only way of defining the ground underneath it.

titanium white   yellow ochre   burnt sienna

cobalt blue   raw umber

1

This painting *(1)* shows a more distant view of the scene in the previous image, the exact relationship being apparent from the marked picture *(4)*. The other major difference is that it is seen in a different season and many changes will occur in a wooded landscape as the trees lose their leaves and the landscape is reduced to a skeletal structure covered in snow. The quality of light is extremely important; the shadows are harsh and cool in tone against the brilliant white of the areas which reflect light fully. The basis of these aspects of the composition are established immediately in the drawing, made with a round hog-hair brush and blue-grey paint well diluted with turpentine.

2

3

4

A broad wash of blue across the foreground represents the heavy shadow (2). By contrast, the elements of warmer tone are added using raw umber for the dark tree trunk and touches of burnt sienna thinly washed in or mixed with white in the line of trees across the background. Horizontal lines clearly establish the receding plane from foreground to background (3). The stark nature of the view is emphasized in this way, unlike the previous composition where the foliage, although sparse, gives density to the landscape. In the final stage the trees are given more definite form with heavy brushmarks in warm and cool greys and pure white. On the horizontal plane the blue shadow is strengthened but remains as an unmodified contrast to the white. Against this fairly plain ground detail is provided by the trees, put in with loose, vigorous brushstrokes. The composition (4) is carefully balanced by the combination of colours, tones and surface texture.

Greek Villas

oil on canvas 36 x 48 inches (91 x 122 cm)

The view from almost directly above this group of little houses enabled the artist to build a composition of diagonal lines, rather than predominant horizontals and verticals. The interest of this subject lies in the maze-like quality of steps, paths and courtyards, all on different levels. The eye is invited to explore the small corners of space, which together seem to make a puzzle. As our attention is led around the canvas, we are constantly coming to a halt on the surface, only to be diverted again by another accent.

The motif was studied on several occasions, the various figures being observed separately. In this sense, the painting is a studio composition, executed at one remove from the subject, the artist having decided to sacrifice the benefits of working on the spot in exchange for having more time to reflect on his original fascinations for the scene. These included the separateness of each square space or courtyard which was at the same time locked with the others in an indivisible whole. The ordinariness of the girls chatting outside a front door, the man and woman working in their yard, and the old woman spinning on her own, somehow seemed to belie the intricacies of the setting.

1

titanium white

lemon yellow

yellow ochre

Naples yellow

burnt sienna

raw umber

cobalt blue

ultramarine

viridian

sap green

alizarin crimson

cadmium red

2

3

This is a complex scene with its jumble of architecture interspersed with foliage and the tonal contrast of deep shadows among the bright buildings *(1)*. The bare outlines of the main features are sketched in with cobalt blue, well diluted with turpentine, and the solid mid-tones of roofs, walls and trees blocked in *(2)*. This basic structure is given more solidity and colour by working across the canvas adding broad patches of tone, mixing white, raw umber and cobalt blue for the greys, burnt sienna and white for the warm tones, and viridian with umber, yellow and cobalt blue to make the greens *(3)*. A medium-sized round hog-hair brush is used. The long handle gives freedom to work each area *(4)* and the stiff bristles add texture to the paint surface *(5)*.

4

5

1

2

4

5

3

In the early stages of an oil painting the colour can be blocked in quickly, filling the basic areas of tone (1) before the paint texture and colour relationships are refined. At first the paint should be applied thinly, diluted with turpentine, and the canvas weave can be seen through the paint which forms a stain of colour on the surface (2) rather than a thick skin. In this way the whole canvas is gradually covered and forms can be developed in more detail. It is a matter of preference which type of brush is used, but on a medium or large canvas bristle brushes are most convenient for blocking in as they are resilient and can be handled freely (3). Although it is important to recreate the subject faithfully a painting can become dull if the materials are not also considered with equal attention. The thickness and texture of the paint and qualities of the brushmarks add vitality (4).

To emphasize an atmosphere of heat and light the warm tones are put in with yellow ochre, white, Naples yellow and burnt sienna (5). Alizarin crimson added to the blue-greys gives them a warm cast in shadow areas. The trees and hedge are built up more solidly with tones of green and more detail is drawn in the house (6).

In the finished painting (7) the colours and tones have been more fully balanced, setting up the contrasts of light and dark, warm and cool which give a vibrant effect to the colours. As thicker paint is added the brushmarks are carefully judged and made to describe the general form and direction of each element, whether organic or manmade. The blue-grey tones offset light, warm yellows and the rich greens of trees and hedge, while the cluster of plants on the balcony adds a splash of colour in the predominant white of the brightly-lit building. The blue, yellow and pink clothes of the figures also provide tiny colour keys in the painting which lead the eye across the composition towards the focal point of the central villa.

6

7

The Cliff at Beachy Head

acrylic on canvasboard 20 x 24 inches (51 x 61 cm)

One of the most frequent problems of painting dramatic, natural formations is how best to give the spectator a feeling of their awe-inspiring scale. Early painters of the English landscape, such as Philip James de Loutherbourg (1740–1812) and Joseph Wright (1734–97), who both painted the rocky landscape of Derbyshire, almost invariably included in their works some small manmade feature, figures or animals, in order to impart this sense of scale. Here the foreshortened view of the lighthouse serves this purpose. It also contributes, with its shadow on the water, to establish the flatness of the sea. This flat surface in turn offsets the rugged, precipitous cliff face, almost inducing a feeling of vertigo. The texture of the chalk cliffs is enhanced by the gently modulated surface of the water as it recedes towards the horizon.

The feeling for the exact quality of surfaces is an important element in this painting. It is achieved to some extent by the brushwork appropriate to each area but also by the careful observation of cast shadows. The hard, dark shadow in the foreground intensifies the dense, chalky white where the sun strikes the cliff face. The small shadow of the lighthouse provides the artist with an opportunity to imply the translucency of the surrounding water. The result is a painting of contrasts; horizontal with vertical, cool with warm. These effects depend heavily on the particular position of the sun. The artist has built the composition around the configuration of shapes at a particular time.

5

1

 light green
 Hooker's green

 yellow ochre
 cadmium yellow

 ultramarine
Payne's gray

 phthalo blue
raw umber

 black
cadmium red

2

3

Acrylics are opaque and quick-drying so colours must be blended quickly or overlaid in thin washes of paint well diluted with water. The sky and sea are first blocked in with graded tones of blue-grey (1). Hooker's green is the basic colour of the grassy clifftop. Details of the rock formation are brushed in (2) emphasizing the tonal contrast of heavy shadows and the reflective white surface. The texture is then roughened by spattering thin paint (3) and this is set against a smooth reworking of sky and sea. Details are refined in the last stage (4) and the lighthouse painted with a small sable brush.

The sky and sea are painted with a mixture of Payne's gray, ultramarine and white with a little yellow oxide added to give a greenish tinge to the sea. Mix acrylic colours in roughly the quantity needed at each stage (5) as unused paint will quickly dry on the palette. The initial blocking in may be done with a broad hog-hair brush to spread the colour quickly, but a No 6 sable gives more precision in following outlines on the cliff and lighthouse (6)

6

Below Spattering is a simple technique which adds to the variety of texture in the painting. A torn piece of newspaper is placed on the painting to mask off the areas of sea and sky. This also provides a rough edge to the spattering, defining the shapes on the cliff face. A broad bristle brush is loaded with well diluted paint and held over the painting. Flicking the bristles with finger and thumb causes drips and blots of colour to fall onto the paint surface. The technique cannot be precisely controlled but the texture can be modified by overpainting

4

Bridge at Richmond

acrylic on canvas 20 x 26 inches (51 x 66 cm)

The forms and shapes of particular bridges observed by painters over the centuries constitute a recurrent theme in the history of landscape painting. Corot, Monet, van Gogh, Whistler, Cézanne and Matisse are just a few of the artists who have made the arches of a bridge an important part, if not actually the main theme, of some of their pictures. In some cases it is the view framed by the bridge, a picture within a picture, which gives the subject its fascination. Or, as with Cezanne, it is the simple geometric value of a Roman arch.

In the painting here, the artist was absorbed by the intricate decorative detail of an iron bridge over the Thames, but at the same time used each arch to form a series of small glimpses within the larger framework of the composition. The whole bridge is given its position in space by the extended foreground, and by the fact that we can see the tops of the distant trees appearing above the bridge. The details of the architecture itself and the intricacies of the lock gates seen through the righthand arch contrast with the simplified treatment of the river bank and the groups of trees in the distance. A further contrast to the architectural shapes is provided by the freer handling of the nearest river bank on the right. The bridge itself, being the main subject for the artist, is placed so that one of its arches sits centrally in the canvas, but as this is not the central arch an over-symmetrical arrangement is avoided.

Acrylic paint is well suited to work which demands areas of flat colour, and also where clean, hard-edged shapes are needed. Both the sky and the patterns made by the architecture of the bridge take advantage of this quality.

Above The painting is executed on cotton duck primed with white acrylic emulsion. This has a slight tooth which grips the paint but does not interfere with the texture. The first wash of colour is a light blue-grey, applied with a bristle brush. The paint is applied thinly and built up in successive layers to modify colour and tone.

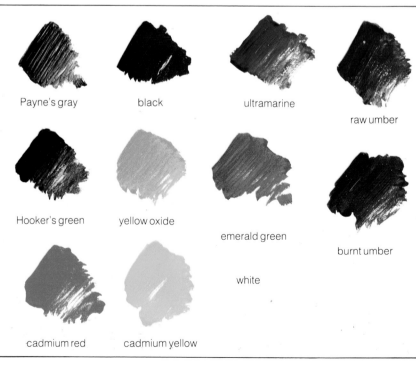

Payne's gray

black

ultramarine

raw umber

Hooker's green

yellow oxide

emerald green

burnt umber

white

cadmium red

cadmium yellow

The basic structure of this composition is quite simple but the bridge itself contains much intricate detail. The shapes are first lightly sketched on the canvas in pencil and the broad areas of sky and water brushed in with grey-blue (1). Trees behind the bridge are put in with a darker grey and the bank and foliage loosely described with raw umber (2). Initially the shapes are not precise so form and colour are gradually developed and modified as the work progresses (3). Flat hog-hair brushes are used to cover the canvas with colour while a medium, round sable brush has a fine point suitable for drawing details of the bridge.

1

Below Acrylics can be overpainted quite rapidly to develop the relationships of colour and tone, but it may be as well to put in the shapes quite precisely from the start. The arch of the bridge is followed with a fine sable brush (below) while broad areas of flat colour are applied with a broad bristle brush (bottom) in long strokes.

2

3

4

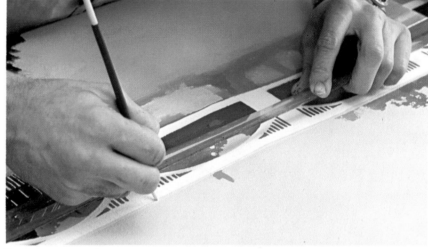

6

5

7

When the basic shapes are established the tones can be adjusted to add definition to various elements in the image. The river is reworked with a lighter colour (4) to emphasize the dark reflection of the bridge. The riverbank is overlaid with Hooker's green and a broad yellow strip is painted across the top of the bridge (5). To paint the horizontal lines accurately the brush is guided along a plastic ruler, held at a slight angle from the surface of the canvas (6).

The structure of the bridge is more carefully defined (7). Light and dark tones of grey, mixed with raw umber and yellow oxide, are used to establish the basic three-dimensional forms. At the same time the bank and reflections in the river are developed. Following this, colours are put in which imitate the paintwork of the bridge (8).

8

9

10

11
Detailed work on the bridge is added with a ïine sable brush, each shape described with great precision and paying careful attention to colour and tone (9). Emerald green, Hooker's green, white and yellow oxide are mixed to form the appropriate colours, shaded with raw umber. Finally the grassy bank is described by drawing lightly with the brush (10). A watercolour sketch for the painting (11) shows the different effect of the more delicate medium compared to acrylic.

A primed hardboard support is used here, which does not grip the paint evenly at first, so a variety of textural effects can be made. The foreground and sky are loosely put in with a broad bristle brush *(1, 7)*. The green in the foreground is brushed with water and blotted with a rag *(6)* to show up the brushmarks. This is contrasted with a flatter area at the horizon *(5)* put in with a flat synthetic bristle brush. When the landscape is blocked in the basic tones of the walls and house are established *(2)* Black, raw umber, white, yellow ochre and Payne's grey are the colours used. The fields behind the house are given flatter colour and more variety of tone. The sky is gradually reworked with blended colour and the foreground given more depth with a wash of dark green and light spatterings of colour *(3)*. At the same time details of the house and its surroundings are gradually developed *(4, 8)*.

4

1

2

3

5

6

7

Heavy Weather

acrylic on hardboard 24 x 27 inches (61 x 69 cm)

This picture is, as the title suggests, primarily concerned with the menace of the elements; however, such sensations can seldom be achieved by simply making the sky dark. Here the white sheets drying on the washing line contribute as much to the final effect as the colour of the threatening clouds above. Firstly they are the lightest shapes in the painting, and the contrast of their whiteness with the predominately dark, surrounding areas gives the colour of the sky more force. Secondly, their foreshortened shapes, as they billow out in the wind in the direction of the spectator, express the force of the wind. These jagged shapes are also related to the regular geometric architectural shapes of the house behind. The house provides an element of stability in the composition, both with its clean vertical and horizontal lines and its placing in relation to the horizon. The line of its roof is an important part of the broad sweep of the horizon itself, despite not being exactly in line. This stability serves to set off the diagonals and irregular shapes elsewhere in the painting: the sheets on the line, the lighted accents in the sky and a similar accent repeated in the grass in the right foreground.

The painting of a foreground in a landscape can often present particular problems. Sometimes the individual shapes of blades of grass or leaves on a tree can be easily discernible, but at a slightly greater distance the artist is forced to make a decision between the elaborate portrayal of minute detail and a way of making a more generalized statement. The best solution is often to start with fairly large masses of colour and then see if more detailed treatment is appropriate as the painting progresses. Here the artist has overlaid a broad area of green with a very free splattering of paint in keeping with the overall feel of the subject. This splattering also serves to introduce a feeling of movement.

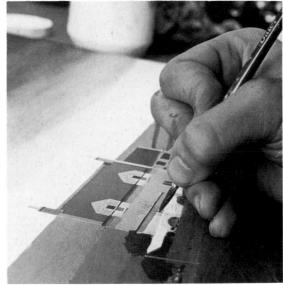

8

Printmaking

Paints, pencils and pens are all materials which the artist can take with him into the landscape. Some methods of making pictures require equipment which is firmly anchored in the studio. Most printmaking techniques come into this category, partly because the nature of the printmaking process involves a chrysalis stage before the work can be completed. This has not prevented printmakers from making a continuous and important contribution to the art of landscape painting. From the time of Hercules Seghers (*c*.1589-*c*.1638), the great landscape etcher of the early seventeenth century, artists have spent many hours in their workshops with wood and metal, burins and acids, waxes and inks, and have produced landscapes of great importance. The following descriptions of printmaking methods explain the basic principles of each technique.

Left *Types of printing*
In relief printing, the surface which creates the printed impression is raised in relief and the rest of the block is cut away. In the intaglio processes, the image is incised in a metal plate. In planographic printing, the image and the undrawn area are on the same level – the process is based on the antipathy of grease and water. In screenprinting, ink is pushed through a mesh or screen. The design is applied to the screen by a masking stencil or by painting out areas with a liquid that sets as a resist.

Right *Landscape with Herdsmen*, Thomas Gainsborough. This print is a soft-ground etching, a technique pioneered in England by Gainsborough and John Crome in the eighteeenth century. A soft wax is laid thinly on the surface of the etching plate, and this is then covered with a fine but strong paper. The drawing is made on the paper and the pressure exerted by the pencil lifts the wax off the plate, exposing the metal wherever the artist has drawn. These lines are then bitten by the acid and eventually print as soft lines similar to those made by a soft pencil or crayon. The method was very appropriate for Gainsborough's lyrical scenes.

Relief printing

This category of prints includes the woodcut, the wood engraving and the linocut. The artist cuts away part of the surface of a flat block of wood or a sheet of lino. The areas which he has left untouched are then covered with printing ink, a sheet of paper is laid on top and pressure is applied to the back of the paper, either in a press or by burnishing it with the back of a spoon. As soon as the paper is lifted off the block, it will be seen that the image has been reversed, as though seen in a mirror; this reversal of the image must be taken into account when planning the composition. Also, it is only the untouched part of the block which receives the ink, so the actual marks cut onto the surface with a knife or gouge will be the negative, or white shapes, of the print.

One of the main differences between drawing or painting and printmaking is that the printmaker cannot avoid considering from the first moment what happens to the whole surface of the block. The good draughtsman will also consider the whole area of his paper, but he can nevertheless make marks without doing so. The printmaker uses the white of the paper as an integral part of his design, rather than as a background on which lines or shapes are superimposed.

The relief print lends itself to bold, simplified images, but it is worth looking at the woodcuts of Albrecht Dürer (1471-1528) and the wood engravings of Thomas Bewick (1753-1828) to see that a wealth of fine detail is also possible. More recently there have been developments of a different nature. Because the ink is applied to the surface of a block, there has been an increasing use of surfaces which themselves have interesting qualities. Any old piece of wood, perhaps with a knot or two in it, can suggest a readymade landscape. Whereas Dürer and Bewick used hard woods which printed the ink evenly, printmakers since then have used softer woods with a more pronounced grain which leaves its own impression on

Right *Trees and Fields* The artist has brought a very light touch to this linocut. One of the main technical challenges of this medium is to cut away the white areas in a way which will not impair the delicacy of the forms. Here the spaces between the branches and the patchwork of fields defined by the hedges that surround them have been carved with great skill and sympathy.

Below The equipment needed for making a linocut is relatively simple. Tracing paper and carbon paper is used to transfer the design to the linoleum. Brushes and paint could be used instead. A knife and gouges are used to cut away the lino, and a roller and inks are used for printing.

Cutting lino
1. Draw the design on the lino in ink or use tracing paper and carbons. Cut straight edges with a knife and ruler.

2. Work towards the knife cut with a small gouge, taking care not to chip away the straight edge.

the paper and can contribute to the final image. Surfaces other than wood – in fact, any surface which can have ink applied to it, paper laid on top of it and be burnished from behind – can be used to obtain a variety of textures.

Relief prints are not limited to black or just one colour. Edvard Munch cut his woodblocks into pieces with a saw, inked each piece separately with a different colour and then reassembled them like a jigsaw puzzle before taking an impression. Another method of colour printing is to print a block in one colour and make another block to print a second colour on top of the first. This method has the advantage that the second block can be cut so that in places it will print where the first one did not, as well as in places on top of the first, so that a third colour will be produced where the two overlap. The Japanese woodcut artists use colour in a different way. Instead of applying the printing ink on the surface with a roller, which is the Western tradition, they painted the ink on with brushes. This requires great skill as the ink has to be a very thin even, film or it will print blotchily.

Below Tools for making woodcuts include gouges for clearing away large areas and V-tools for cutting lines. A knife can be used to cut outlines directly. All tools should be sharpened regularly on an oilstone.

3. Steady the block with one hand, well out of the way of the gouge for safety. Use a larger gouge for cutting away broad areas.

4. A broad gouge will remove more lino. Shallow cuts leave an area of texture; deep cuts show white on the print.

5. Experiment with cutting tools to create a variety of surfaces and textures.

6. A small V-shaped gouge will make fine lines.

7. A U-shaped gouge will make broad lines. Control all tools carefully to avoid sudden slips which could give unwanted marks.

The basic materials needed for relief printing are a piece of lino or a piece of wood with a moderately flat surface, and tools for cutting the surface. These are shaped either as a V or rounded as a gouge, but some woodcutters just use a sharp knife. Printing ink, which can be bought in tubes, should preferably be oil-based as the water-based ones tend to separate while still in the tube. Paper should be strong, but light and absorbent. There are some imitation Japanese papers which are ideal for the final prints, but proofs can be taken on much cheaper ones while the work is still in progress. A roller for applying the ink can be rubber or plastic but should be soft enough to allow for the surface of the block not being absolutely flat. A press is a great advantage, but they are scarce and expensive. For small prints a good impression can be made with the back of a large spoon or other smooth rounded object.

Wood engraving Rather more specialized tools are needed for a wood engraving. A woodcut is made on the "plank" of the wood with the grain running across the surface, whereas a wood engraving uses the end grain. Trees with a very slow rate of growth provide the most suitable wood for this purpose as the rings are very close together. Pear and holly are often used, but the best is boxwood. The blocks must be prepared by a skilled craftsman, as the surface must be absolutely flat and smooth. This hard, smooth surface is receptive to the most delicate touch of the cutting tool and is capable of reproducing the finest detail. The tools used are similar to small chisels and come in different shapes. The basic principles of printing are the same as for woodcuts or linocuts.

Intaglio printing

In relief printing the part of the surface which is removed is the part which does not print. In intaglio printing it is the other way round. Designs are incised into thin metal plates, which can be highly polished and which are capable of withstanding great press-

ure. A thick printing ink is rubbed all over the surface so that it will fill up the parts which have been eaten by acid or cut away with a sharp tool. The surface, which is very smooth, is then wiped clean, leaving the ink in the incisions untouched. The plate is taken to the press and placed on the "bed", a steel plank which passes between two steel rollers. The paper, which must be strong and elastic and softened with water, is put on top of the plate, and soft felt blankets on top of the paper. This is wound through the rollers of the press, similar to a mangle, and the great pressure exerted through the felt blankets moulds the paper to the form of the plate. The ink which lies below the surface is lifted out by the paper.

The moulding of the paper to the form of the plate quite literally gives an intaglio print an extra dimension. Not only do the inked areas stand up from the paper's surface, because they were below the surface of the plate, but also the paper which overlapped the edges of the plate will be higher than the image itself.

Below *Cat at Window*, Hiroshige (1797–1858). This Japanese print was made from a single printing, using a technique known as rainbow inking. The plate is inked with all the different colours so that only one printing is required. Japanese prints began to appear in Europe at the end of the nineteenth century and had a great influence on artists such as Henri de Toulouse-Lautrec (1864–1901).

Below Some of the tools used for wood engraving include flat, round, lozenge and burin engravers. Wood engravings are made by cutting into the end grain of wood and the tools are closer to those used by copper and steel engravers than those used by woodcutters.

Left *Audley End* (1973), Edward Bawden (b. 1903). This print was taken from a linocut and illustrates well the graphic possibilities of the medium. Characteristic linocut marks have been exploited for their decorative and textural effects, especially on the path, border and trees. The print was made using five blocks and five colours, one for each block.

Below *Autumn Eve, Lamorna* This print is a combination of two intaglio techniques: etching and aquatint. It was printed using two plates and four colours. Both techniques were combined on each plate and two colours were used on each.

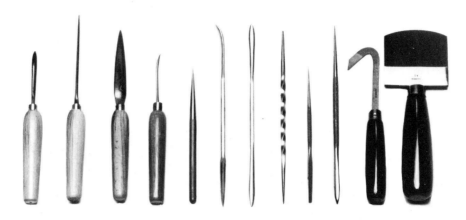

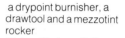

Above A variety of tools are needed for the different techniques in intaglio printing. These include *(left to right)*: short and long burnishers; flat, curved and pointed burnishers; a burnisher and scraper; a double edged burnisher; a pointed and flat burnisher; a drypoint burnisher, a drawtool and a mezzotint rocker

Below *Harbour Defences* A whole range of intaglio techniques have been used to produce this print, which is distinguished by its subtle range of tones and evocative detail.

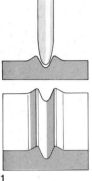

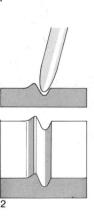

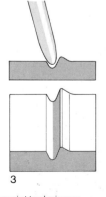

Drypoint techniques
1. If the needle is held upright, the burr will erupt evenly on both sides of the line.
2, 3. If the needle is held at an angle, then the burr will rise unevenly on one side of the line.

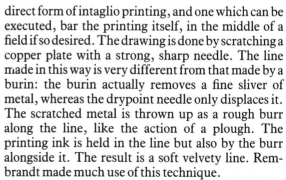

Engraving The engraving is the oldest form of intaglio print. It requires simple equipment but considerable skill. The metal used is normally copper, which is cut with a tool called the burin. The burin is a short steel rod, square in section, cut off at an angle to form an extremely sharp point. The other end is fitted into a small wooden handle which fits into the palm of the hand. Lines are cut in the copper by pushing the burin forwards. Slight variations in the angle at which it is held will determine the thickness and depth of the line. It takes strong fingers and much practice to achieve any degree of control, and the burin must always be kept sharp. The great reward of this medium is the sinuous, pure and incisive quality of the line produced.

Drypoint This is in many ways the simplest and most direct form of intaglio printing, and one which can be executed, bar the printing itself, in the middle of a field if so desired. The drawing is done by scratching a copper plate with a strong, sharp needle. The line made in this way is very different from that made by a burin: the burin actually removes a fine sliver of metal, whereas the drypoint needle only displaces it. The scratched metal is thrown up as a rough burr along the line, like the action of a plough. The printing ink is held in the line but also by the burr alongside it. The result is a soft velvety line. Rembrandt made much use of this technique.

Etching Etching is the printmaking medium which has always held the greatest interest for landscape artists, many of whom used it for their best work. It is probable that etching was first evolved by engravers

such as Dürer, who sought a greater freedom than the line made by the burin could offer. Etching is a process where acid, rather than a burin, is used to remove the metal. Dürer's etchings clearly reveal his debt to engraving, but he did not use the medium in Hercules Seghers' particularly inventive way a century later. It was in the hands of Seghers and Rembrandt that etching was born as a medium in its own right, soon to be adopted by Claude, Canaletto and a succession of great landscape artists.

The traditional method is to coat the metal plate, which is usually made of copper, but sometimes zinc or steel, with an acid-resistant film. Beeswax is the main ingredient of this film. The drawing is made by scratching the wax from the surface with a needle, so exposing the metal underneath. This need not be

done in the studio; the plate can easily be carried outdoors but it must be remembered that the final print will come out as a mirror-image of the drawing.

After the drawing is made, access to an etching workshop is essential. The plate is put into a dish of acid, which eats away the metal where the wax has been removed. The longer the plate stays in the acid, the more metal will be eaten away and the deeper the lines will become. When the plate is removed from the acid, the wax film is cleaned off and a print is made in the same way as an engraving. Lines which have been "bitten" by the acid for a long time will hold a lot of the printing ink and will show as strong dark lines on the paper. Equally, very pale lines will result from a short time in the acid. This way of being able to control and vary the strength of a line has given

Above *Black Lion Wharf*, James McNeill Whistler (1834–1903). Whistler first learnt about printmaking when he worked as a naval cartographer. Born in America, he came to Europe and was instrumental in establishing etching in England as a more interesting medium for artists than the reproductive role it had previously occupied. His everyday London river scenes, as here, also stressed the aesthetic qualities of an artist's work in reaction to the emphasis on subject matter.

Above Individual proofs are taken of each of the colours as well as sequence prints. These proofs enable the printer and the artist to check how the different inks are taking and make fine adjustments.

Colour lithography
To make a colour lithograph, a great deal of patience and concentration is required to achieve a result which corresponds to the artist's original intentions. A number of lithographic stones or plates are prepared, drawn with the areas which correspond to the different colours of the final design. These are then inked with the appropriate colours and printed in sequence. Accurate registration is crucial. Getting the colour balance right often means altering the sequence in which the colours are imposed; reproofing may be necessary. Progressives, or sequence prints, *(left)* are an essential aid to the artist. These prints, taken at various stages of the colour imposition help the artist to understand the anatomy of the work and decide where to make any changes that might be necessary. The final print *(above)* has a colour key in the margin showing the order in which the various colours have been printed.

Top *The Large Tree*,
Hercules Seghers (1589–c.
1638). Seghers was a Dutch
artist who made many
landscape etchings. His
techniques were innovative
and he exerted a
considerable influence on
Rembrandt's approach to
the medium. He was most
notable for the freedom he
brought to his etchings, at
this time still a young art-form
and much influenced by the
harder, drier line produced
by engravers.

Above This etching was
produced using only two
plates to give the wide variety
of tones: one for yellow and
one for blue-grey. Orange
was also added to the lower
part of the yellow plate. The
artist has expanded this
range further by using the
white of the paper in a
positive way for the
gateposts.

etching a much valued flexibility and expressive
power, as Rembrandt realized early on. One way to
achieve this variety of tone is to draw all the lines on
the plate, whatever their eventual intended strength.
The plate is put in the acid for a short time and then
removed. The lines which are to be pale are then
covered with an acid-resistant varnish and the plate is
put back in the acid so that the remaining lines
become deeper.

Another version of this method involves the lines
on a plate all being bitten, the wax film or "ground"
removed, and a print taken. Another ground is then
applied and more lines drawn and bitten in the acid,
either to a similar or different depth. Rembrandt
worked in this way, constantly adding to and altering
the previous drawing, the print gaining in richness at
each stage.

Another way of manipulating the final result,
and a field where there is constant experiment, is the
use of different materials to resist the acid where the
metal plate is to remain unbitten. Any material which

Left *Twilight with Haystacks* (1879), Camille Pissarro. Pissarro was both prolific and very versatile, but also very consistent in his approach. His etching closely follows the style of his painting. Although the process of making an etching is broken down into various stages, this print shows that there need be no loss of the spontaneity of sensation which Pissarro considered so important.

is not attacked by acid can be appropriate, from resin varnishes to adhesive plastic film. A variation which has advantages for the landscape artist is to cover the plate with a very soft wax which remains sticky. This is covered with a piece of paper on which a drawing is made. The pressure exerted by the pencil will lift the soft wax from the surface of the plate wherever a line has been drawn. The appeal of this technique is that the lines made in this way are much softer, more like a chalk drawing, than those produced with a needle scratched into a harder wax. Again, the plate can be carried away from the studio and the drawing made direct from the motif.

Aquatint Drypoint and etching are the most direct ways of drawing lines on the plate. If the artist wishes to work with shapes or areas instead, this can be done with aquatint. This name is used because the effect is similar to that of a wash drawing. Aquatint exploits the fact that any roughness on the surface of the plate will hold the printing ink, whereas the smooth areas will be wiped clean. The rougher the surface, the

more ink will be held and the darker this will print on the paper. This roughness is achieved by sprinkling finely powdered resin or bitumen onto the plate, which is then heated sufficiently for the tiny grains to melt and stick to the surface. Any part of the plate which is to remain white is covered with an acid-resistant varnish. The plate then goes into the acid which eats tiny holes into the surface in between the grains of resin. If it is kept in the acid a long time the holes will get deeper, and the surface will consequently be rougher. This will result in a darker, possibly even black, area when the ink is applied. The process can be broken down into stages, as when making lines of different depths. If the resultant area is too dark, it can be rubbed with charcoal or a tool called a burnisher to make it smoother, so it will hold less ink.

These methods are just a few ways of making marks on a plate. They can all be combined together on the same plate if desired, and there is really no limit to the range of textures that the inventive artist can

Bottom *Patmos Walls* In this screenprint, the artist has expressed delight at the tiny glimpse of landscape set like a window within large areas of wall. The rough texture on the wall was achieved by laying a screen over a paving stone and then rubbing candle wax over the top to pick up the texture. The wax acts as a stencil and is consequently incorporated.

Right *Am See* This delicate lithograph was executed on a plate, rather than a lithographic stone. The artist used washes applied with an airbrush to achieve these atmospheric effects.
Bottom right *Approach of Night* (1910), Alfred Hartley (1855–1933). The hazy effect of evening mist has been achieved in this print with the use of aquatint.

Below *Harvest* This screenprint was printed using hand-painted stencils. Fine detail is possible with this technique and the result is an effective impression of a late summer landscape.

discover for himself. Coloured inks can be used that are even more brilliant than the colours available to the painter. The method of making a coloured etching which gives most control and scope for variation is to have a separate plate for each colour. The plates are all inked ready for printing and then taken through the press in quick succession. This is necessary because the paper, being dampened to make it soft and malleable, shrinks as it dries. A simpler way of adding colour to an etching is to treat the plate like a linocut or woodcut, and apply a second colour, once the first has been rubbed into the lines.

Lithography

Lithography is a more recent development than either the woodcut or etching. It was invented in 1798 by Aloïs Senefelder (1771-1834) and, unlike relief or intaglio printing, the surface is not cut or corroded away. Lithography is based on the principle that grease and water repel each other. The drawing is made with a greasy crayon or ink onto a porous, even-grained surface. This surface is traditionally a particular sort of limestone from Bavaria, but for the sake of easier manipulation, sheets of zinc or aluminium are now prepared to simulate the grain of the original stones.

The whole surface is dampened with water, which lies evenly on the areas where there is no grease. A printing roller charged with an oil-based ink is pushed over the stone or zinc plate, and the grease left by the drawing will attract the ink, but the water elsewhere will repel it. The printing paper is then laid on top and it is taken through a specially constructed press. Once the print is made the stone can be quickly inked again ready for the next.

Lithography has been most consistently popular in France. It was used early on by the romantic artists Eugène Delacroix, who was born in the same year as lithography itself, and Jean Louis Gericault; later it was explored by the Impressionists, with particular effect by Edouard Vuillard (1868-1940) and Pierre Bonnard (1867-1947).

Screenprinting

Screenprinting, sometimes called silkscreen, is a sophisticated form of stencil. The stencil, whatever form it takes, is applied to a fine mesh or screen which is stretched over a frame. The screen can be made of a variety of materials from real silk to nylon or metal. Once the stencil is in place the screen is placed over a sheet of paper and a fairly liquid ink is forced through the screen with a strip of plastic called a squeegee. The stencils will block the passage of ink through the screen, leaving those areas of the paper white. Stencils can be put directly onto the screen in the form of liquids, which will set hard, or indirectly by preparing the shapes separately and then glueing them to the screen. There is much scope for the artist to exercise his ingenuity in the creation of stencils appropriate to his work, bearing in mind that the stencil must be made from a material which will not be dissolved or destroyed by the ink he uses. The basic equipment can be very simple.

2

3

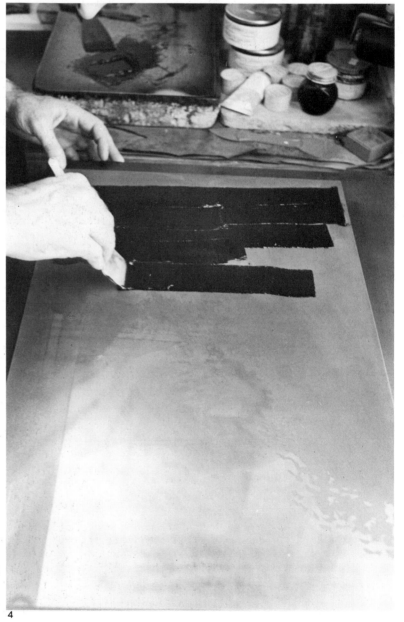

1

4

5

Making an etching
Gentle variations and gradations of tone can be achieved in an aquatint by burnishing the surface of the plate in order to make it smoother and consequently hold less ink *(1)*. The tool used here also has a scraper at the other end. This is used for the more radical removal of unwanted marks. Ink for printing etchings must have a very particular consistency *(2, 3)*. It must be stiff enough to remain in the lines or textures bitten by the acid into the plate's surface, and yet it must not be so sticky that it cannot be wiped easily off the surface. Many artists prefer to make their own ink from dry pigments so that the consistency can be controlled and varied for particular needs. For most purposes, the best test of the ink's viscosity is to let it fall off the knife to ascertain if it is too runny. The next stage is when the ink is spread over the plate *(4)*, taking care to ensure that all parts are well filled. The ink is then wiped off the surface of the plate with large pads of tarlatan *(5)*. The printer avoids using

excessive downward pressure so that no ink will be pulled out of the bitten areas. Broad sweeps take most of the ink off, and are then followed by rapid circular polishing. Clean pieces of tarlatan are used for the final stages. The printer aims to wipe the plate as evenly as possible so that no parts of the plate hold more ink than the artist intended them to *(6)*. The plate is now ready to be put on the bed of the press. The paper, softened by damping, is placed over the plate, with felt blankets placed over the paper. As the plate is wound through the press, the felt blankets push the soft paper into the lines or textures which are holding the ink *(7)*. The print is then made, but it must be dried under a flat board with considerable weight on top to ensure that the paper will not cockle as it dries. If another print is to be made immediately, the plate is inked up again in the same fashion. Otherwise, the plate must be cleaned thoroughly so that any ink left in the lines will not dry there.

7

6

Left *Sleeping Woman Mountain* This print is made solely with aquatint. It exploits the strong tonal contrasts that occur when the sun is low on the horizon and strikes only the highest features of the landscape. On this occasion, the artist wanted to avoid the normal reversal of the image which take place when making a print. This is done by making drawings and then tracing the final one. The tracing is then turned over before placing it on the plate so that all the work on the plate is in the form of a mirror-image. This ensures that the finished print will be the right way round.

GLOSSARY
INDEX
CONTRIBUTING ARTISTS
ACKNOWLEDGEMENTS

GLOSSARY

Aquatint
An etching technique which gives areas of tone, made up of many tiny holes bitten into the plate's surface.

Body colour
A watercolour paint which has been made opaque by the addition of white. Also known as gouache or poster paint.

Burnisher
A tool used in etching to reduce the roughness, or ink-holding properties on a plate.

Chiaroscuro
The use of contrasting light and dark areas in a painting. It is a term now mostly applied to paintings where this contrast is particularly strong, such as those of Rembrandt or Caravaggio.

Complementary colours
If the colours of the spectrum are arranged in a circle, with the three primaries equally spaced, the complementary is the colour which is opposite another in this circle. Green opposite red, for example.

Collage
A picture made by sticking materials such as cloth or paper onto the surface of the canvas.

Dipper
A small container for oil or turpentine. Many types clip onto the palette, and the best have screw tops.

Fixative
A thin varnish applied to pastel or charcoal in order to hold it on the paper and obviate smudging. It is best applied by spraying.

Fresco
A method of wall-painting perfected in Italy in the sixteenth century. A water-based pigment is painted onto moist plaster which absorbs the colour. It has great permanence.

Fugitive colour
A colour which will either fade or darken with time.

Glaze
A transparent film of paint which, when painted over another colour, will change and enrich it but not obscure it.

Golden Section
A canon of geometric proportion, used by some artists since classical times.

Ground
The prepared surface on which a painting is made. It can be varied in texture, colour and absorbency.

Intaglio print
A print taken from a plate where the ink is held below the surface.

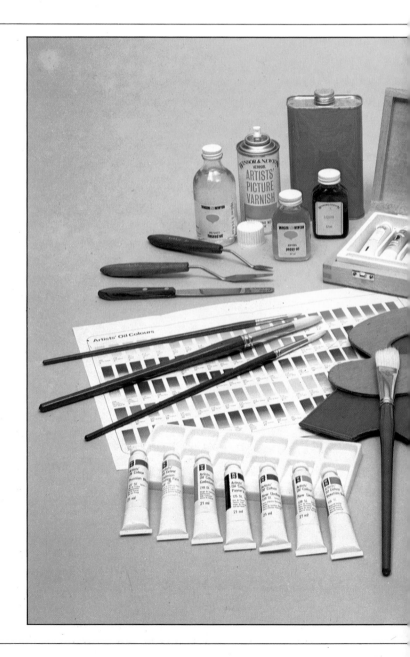

Local colour
The colour of an object, immodified by atmospheric or particular lighting conditions. The normal local colour of grass is green although it may appear pale blue if seen from a great distance.

Medium
This has two meanings for the artist. One refers to the form of pigment he uses, for example oil paint or charcoal. The other is the additive used with the pigment, for example oil and turpentine with oil paint, and gum and water with watercolour.

Modelling
In painting and drawing, modelling is the artist's representation of three-dimensional forms on a flat surface so that they have an apparent solidity. It expresses the artist's understanding of form.

Motif
The artist's chosen subject or image.

Nap
The natural roughness on the surface of a sheet of handmade paper.

Opaque
The opposite of transparent.

Palette
Besides being the surface on which a painter places and mixes his paints, this can also refer to the range of colours he uses.

Permanence
When applied to paints this refers to their ability always to remain the same colour, in normal conditions.

Picture plane
The area of space which the artist has chosen to transfer onto the flat shape of his canvas.

Pigment
The raw materials from which painters' colours are made. They are now both organic and inorganic. The word is also used to mean paint and colour.

Primary colours
The three primary colours are red, yellow and blue, from which in theory all other colours can be made. Secondary colours are made from two primaries, for example green is made from yellow and blue.

Priming
The first coat of pigment in the preparation of a painting surface is the primer. It is normally preceded only by a coat of size.

Relief print
A print taken from a block or plate where the ink has been applied to the highest surface.

Retarder
Anything added to a paint to reduce its drying time. There are many preparations available for all sorts of paint. Some painters of the Renaissance used honey.

Size
A thin glue, frequently made from rabbits' skin, used to protect fibres from the rotting effect of the linseed oil in paint.

Stretcher
The wooden frame on which a painter's canvas is stretched.

Support
The base material on which a picture is made. Canvas, wood or card are the most common.

Topographic
Descriptive of a particular place.

Tonal value
The relative position in a scale between black and white.

Vanishing point
The imaginary point within any one view at which parallel lines appear to converge.

Wash
A very dilute, transparent colour. It usually refers to watercolour which has been mixed with a lot of water.

INDEX

Figures in italics refer to illustrations

D

E

F

L   M   N   O

P

Q

CONTRIBUTING ARTISTS

Diana Armfield   74-5, 76-9, 80-1
Adrian Bartlett   35, 45(t), 58-9, 60-1, 64-5, 106(t), 114-5, 116-7, 118-21, 146
Victoria Bartlett   34(b), 36, 36-7, 37(b)
John Brewer   47
Oliver Campion   107, 108-9
Michael Carlo   142(t)
William Delafield Cook   113
Moira Clinch   37(c), 51(t), 52-3
John Devane   52
Tim Gibbs   111(t)
Maggi Hambling   51(r), 54-5(t), 72-3
Dermot Holland   132-3
Jane Joseph   56-7(t)
Jeremy King   138-9
Thomas Kruger   142-3(t)
Judith Lang   44-5, 46(t), ,47(t), 48, 57, 100
James Marks   44 (tl and bl)
Judy Martin   38(t), 42, 43, 45(b)
Frances Parker   40(l), 41, 62-3
John Raynes   33
Mary Rodd   140(b)
Ian Sidaway   90-1, 122-3, 124-7, 128-9
Stan Smith   87, 89
Raymond Spurrier   142(b)
Alyson Stoneman   135(b)
Lawrence Toynbee   70
Ann Verney   92-5, 96-9, 101-3
Mark Wickham   54-5(b), 111(b)
Marc Winer   53(t)

Key (t)top, (b)bottom, (l)left, (r)right, (c)centre

ACKNOWLEDGEMENTS

The illustrations on these pages were reproduced by courtesy of the following:

6, 7 (Ronald Sheridan's Photo Library); **8** The British Library; **9** The Louvre, Paris; **10** The Trustees, The National Gallery, London; **11(t)** The Louvre (photo Bulloz); **11(b)** The Metropolitan Museum of Art, New York, Rogers Fund, 1919 (photo Eric Pollitzer); **12(t)** The National Gallery, London; **12(b)** Isabella Stewart Gardner Museum, Boston; **13(t)** The Metropolitan Museum of Art, New York, Bequest of Benjamin Altman, 1913; **14** Duke of Buccleuch and Queensberry, Bowhill Collection (photo Royale Publications); **14-15** The Royal Academy, London; **15, 16-17** Victoria and Albert Museum, London; **17** Courtauld Institute of Art, London, Witt Collection; **18(t)** The Tate Gallery, London; **18(b)** The National Gallery of Victoria, Felton Bequest 1937; **18-19** The National Gallery, London; **20** The Phillips Collection, Washington (photo Bridgeman Art Library); **21** The Art Gallery of South Australia, Adelaide (photo Australian Information Service, London); **22** The Hermitage, Leningrad (photo Bridgeman Art Library); **23(t)** The National Gallery, London; **23(c)** Dallas Museum of Fine Arts; **23(b)** Marlborough Fine Art, London; **24** Williams College Museum of Art, Williamstown, Massachusetts; **24-25** Collection Haags Gemeentemuseum, The Hague; **26** Musees Royaux, Brussels; **26-27** The National Gallery, London; **27** Victoria and Albert Museum, London; **29(t)** reproduced by gracious permission of Her Majesty the Queen; **29(b)** Fogg Art Museum, Harvard University, Bequest of Grenville L. Winthrop; **30** The British Museum (photo John Freeman); **30-31** The National Gallery, London; **31** The Tate Gallery, London; **33(b)**, **34(t)** Victoria and Albert Museum; **34(c)** Quarto Publishing Limited; **38(b)** Art Institute of Chicago; **39(t)** The National Gallery, London; **39(b)** The Louvre, Paris (photo Snark); **40-41** Victoria and Albert Museum, London; **46(r)** private collection, London (photo Walter Rawlings); **49(t)** Fitzwilliam Museum, Cambridge; **49(bl)** Albertina, Vienna; **49(br)** Victoria and Albert Museum; **51(b)**, **53(tr)**, **54(l)**, **55**, **56-7(b)**, **67(t)** Q.E.D. Publishing Limited; **67(b)** The British Museum (photo John Freeman); **68** Q.E.D. Publishing Limited; **69** Victoria and Albert Museum, London; **72(b)** Q.E.D. Publishing Limited; **83(t)** The British Museum; **85** The Tate Gallery, London; **88-89**, **104(b)**, **105(b)** Q.E.D. Publishing Limited; **106(b)** The National Gallery, London; **107(r)**, **109(b)**, **110(l)**, **112** Q.E.D. Publishing Limited; **113(t)** The Redfern Gallery/Art International; **130-31** The British Museum; **132-3(b)**, **134(l)** Q.E.D. Publishing Limited; **134(r)** Jarrold Printing Norwich; **135(t)** and b) Christie's Contemporary Art Limited; **136** Imperial War Museum; **137** The Mansell Collection; **140(t)** Rijksmuseum, Amsterdam; **140-41** The Ashmolean Museum, Oxford; **143(b)** Victoria and Albert Museum.

Key (t)top, (b)bottom, (l)left, (r) right, (c) centre